Wisdom to Live By

Wisdom to Live By

Henry Gariepy

VICTOR BOOKS®

A DIVISION OF SCRIPTURE PRESS PUBLICATIONS INC.
USA CANADA ENGLAND

Unless otherwise noted, Scripture quotations are from
the *Holy Bible, New International Version* © 1973, 1978,
1984, International Bible Society. Used by permission of
Zondervan Bible Publishers. Other quotations are from
The New King James Version (NKJV), © 1979, 1980, 1982,
Thomas Nelson, Inc., Publishers; the *King James Version* (KJV); *The Amplified New Testament* (AMP), © 1954,
1958 by the Lockman Foundation; New American Standard Bible (NASB), © the Lockman Foundation, 1960,
1962, 1963, 1968, 1971, 1972, 1973, 1975, 1977; *The New
Testament in Modern English* (PH), Revised Edition, ©
J.B. Phillips, 1958, 1960, 1972, permission of Macmillan
Publishing Co. and Collins Publishers; *The Living Bible*
(TLB), © 1971, Tyndale House Publishers, Wheaton, IL
60189. Used by permission.

Library of Congress Cataloging-in-Publication Data

Gariepy, Henry.
     Wisdom to live by / Henry Gariepy.
          p.   cm.
     Includes index.
     ISBN 0-89693-037-8
     1. Wisdom literature — Prayer-books and devotions —
English.
     I. Title.
BS1455.G29   1991
242'.5–dc20   91-3308
                                                                    CIP

---

1 2 3 4 5 6 7 8 9 10 Printing/Year 95 94 93 92 91

For information, address Victor Books, P.O. 1825, Wheaton, Illinois 60189

Contents

WORDS OF WISDOM FROM THE
BOOK OF ECCLESIASTES

*Dedicated to
Our Children*

*Stephen
Priscilla
Elisabeth
Kathryn*

*Whom God used as His tutors
for the deeper lessons of life,
love, forgiveness, joy, and trust*

F o r e w o r d

Henry Gariepy has given his readers a classic exposition of the wisdom literature of the Old Testament. His book, *Wisdom to Live By,* is as practical as the universal needs of humanity and as modern as tomorrow. This is the seventh in a series of books from the pen of one of America's foremost inspirational writers today.

Wisdom to Live By is an inspiring work, consisting of 100 devotional expositions from Proverbs, Ecclesiastes, and the Song of Songs. The author has selected representative key passages from each, exploring their central truths.

Humanity today is in possession of the greatest amount of knowledge ever accumulated but impoverished by the lack of true wisdom. Modern man has confused knowledge (Greek, *gnosis*), factual information, with wisdom (Greek, *sophia*), which is "the highest intellectual gift of comprehensive insight into the ways and purposes of God . . . that endowment of heart and mind which is needed for the right conduct of life" (Alexander Souter, *A Pocket Lexicon to the New Testament*).

American philosopher Will Durant once said, "Science tells us how to heal and how to kill; it reduces the death rate in retail and then kills us wholesale in war; but only wisdom—desire coordinated in the light of all experience—can tell us when to heal and when to kill."

Gariepy has effectively endowed aphorisms of the Bible's wisdom literature with modern insight and application. Here are timeless truths, tested and proved by the ages, presented in timely terms. What one has said concerning the Book of Proverbs may equally characterize this work: "This book [Proverbs] represents the common sense approach to life and faith. It touches the sacred concerns of all who receive the gift of life and struggle how to live with it. . . . The book distills the theological substance of the Old Testament religion into its practical essence" (C. Hassel Bullock, *An Introduction to the Old Testament Poetic Books*).

This is a practical devotional book that no one can afford to be without, for *Wisdom to Live By* is today's greatest need.

Charles W. Carter,
Scholar-in-Residence, Indiana Wesleyan University

Introduction

Today we are drowning in a sea of information but starving for wisdom. The media overload of the outer world incessantly impinges on us while the inner world all too often remains unexplored and unknown. Everywhere uncertainties abound, and like the dove after the Deluge, we seem to find no solid ground for the soles of our feet.

In this era, married to atomic energy for better or worse till death do us part, true wisdom is no longer an option. It is a life-or-death matter. We run the risk of becoming technical giants but ethical infants. Our survival as a society and as a planet — and our adequacy for living out our faith daily — requires a wisdom that transcends mere human understanding. God has made a provision.

The wisdom literature, a unique portion of the Bible, contains the greatest selection of wise counsel ever given to man. The books of Proverbs, Ecclesiastes, and Song of Songs are the core of this genre and offer rich insight and inspiration for everyday living. In this day of the relativization of values, these books call us back to God's wisdom for the practical realities of life that we meet head-on every day.

Proverbs presents to us the wisdom of God for daily

living. Its moral maxims put religion into the arena of daily relationships. These capsules of truth present a much needed relational theology. They call us to an authentic faith that is woven through the fabric of the routine and commonplace that make up the tapestry of life.

Ecclesiastes is one of the most fascinating books of Scripture. Its pessimistic eloquence is unmatched in the Bible. It launches the reader on an odyssey of the spirit that requires courage as it probes the deepest doubts and questions of life. Its search for meaning leads us down picturesque paths of discovery and vast frontiers of faith. The serious reader is led beyond the book's disconsolate passages to a hard-won affirmation in the "conclusion of the matter."

Whereas Ecclesiastes focuses on man's intellect, the Song of Songs probes man's emotions. It records a contemplation on love. This often neglected book has a special message for an age that has popularized infidelity, rejected the pure instinct of love and brought marriage into disrepute. For our day when lust is often identified with love, there are beautiful insights to be gleaned from this incomparable love song of the Bible.

The wisdom of the Bible is not an elective in the school of life. It is a required course if we are to live purposefully, triumphantly, and eternally. To miss out on the wisdom of these books is to flunk life itself.

Wisdom to Live By focuses on 100 texts from these three books for exposition and application to life. May you glean a new understanding from these timeless texts and apply it to the practical concerns of Christian living.

Section One

WORDS OF WISDOM
FROM PROVERBS

ONE

WORDS OF WISDOM

The proverbs of Solomon . . .
for attaining wisdom and discipline;
for understanding words of insight (1:1-2).

Proverbs is the wisdom book of the Bible and of the ages. Its 915 verses contain the greatest selection of moral maxims and wise counsel ever assembled into a single work.

Proverbs is a book not only for the study, but for the kitchen, the living room, the bedroom, the office, the marketplace. Its teachings and insights apply to the realm of the commonplace. It puts religion into working clothes. It injects spiritual truths into everyday relationships and the routine business of life. The tests of our faith occur at just such intersections as found in these pages.

The down-to-earth practicality of Solomon's sayings seems remote from the otherworldly visions of John the Seer or the theological flights of the Apostle Paul. But down-to-earth is where we must live out the great truths of theology. They must be applied to how we manage our business, our time, ourselves.

When writing his Living Bible paraphrase of Proverbs, Kenneth Taylor concluded, "No other [portions of the Word] have such exciting, thoughtful wisdom as the Proverbs."

Billy Graham testifies: "For a number of years, I have made it a practice to read five psalms and one chapter of Proverbs a day. The Psalms teach us how to get along with God, and the Proverbs teach us how to get along with our fellowmen. . . . Reading this much in each book regularly takes me through them once each month. You cannot imagine the blessing this encounter with the Scriptures has been in my life, especially in recent years."[1]

Charles Swindoll also eulogizes: "Proverbs is the single most practical and helpful book in all the Bible, . . . a volume loaded with capsules of truth that face life head-on. . . . I have never (and I mean never) opened my Bible to Proverbs without finding a 'nugget' or principle or insight that gave me just what I needed at the moment. This book is not only wise, it is relevant and timely, . . . constantly up to date."[2]

Let us discover from this book of wisdom insights that will enrich and enhance our lives, and God's blueprint for life and conduct. May our devotional meditations help us "adorn the doctrine" by application of its timeless truths and teachings.

"Lord, give us light Thy truth to see,
And make us wise in knowing Thee."
— Thomas Pollack

T W O
VITAL RELIGION

[Proverbs] for acquiring a disciplined and prudent life, doing what is right and just and fair (1:3).

If perhaps you have never found Proverbs with its unconnected aphorisms a book to which you are drawn, this may be the time when you discover its rich insights that can change your life. Proverbs will help you apply religion where it counts—in the family, in work and business, in care of your health, and in your relationship with others and with God.

A man lived alone in a mountain cottage who was considered especially wise. Many efforts failed to trick him. One day a proud young man said to himself, "I will surely find something to ask this wise man of the mountain that he will not be able to answer." So he caught a live bird and holding it in his hand went up to the man of the mountain. He asked the sage if the bird were alive or dead. He intended, if the wise man answered "dead" to open his hand and let the bird fly away. If the answer were "alive," he would crush its life in his hand. Either way, he would fool the sage. Thus he came and presented his question. But the old man, perceiving the young man's trickery, answered, "As thou wilt, young man, as thou wilt."

As we cross the threshold of this treasure trove of Proverbs, we are encountering the wisdom of the ages. In our age of knowledge explosion, we can never be superior to the timeless teachings of this great book. May we approach it with receptive minds and hearts and incarnate its wisdom in our daily living.

Lord, let Your Word be "a lamp to my feet and a light for my path."

THREE
THE WISDOM OF SOLOMON

*Let the wise listen and add to their learning,
and let the discerning get guidance (1:5).*

The Book of Proverbs introduces us to over 100 different types of people, including 46 types of men, 23 types of women, several kinds of children, and types that represent both genders. It takes up such themes as honesty, industry, thrift, discretion, humility, pride, boasting, pleasure, temperance, strong drink, truthfulness, immorality, prostitution, wealth, poverty, justice, gossip, family.

Solomon drew many of his proverbs from his knowledge of the natural world. His chronicler wrote: "He spoke of trees . . . also of animals, of birds, of creeping things, and of fish" (1 Kings 4:33, NKJV). All these flora and fauna are found in Proverbs except for fish. His pages teem with object lessons from the bears, lions, oxen, dogs, goats, horses, badgers, donkeys, serpents, ants, bees, birds, cock and eagle.

The contents of Proverbs defy orderly arrangement. The random selection usually offers no connection between adjacent verses. Major themes are interspersed throughout, but mostly treated in isolated verses.

Most of the proverbs originated with Solomon, as attributed within the book (1:1; 10:1; 25:1). His biographer records: "He spoke 3,000 proverbs and his songs numbered 1,005" (1 Kings 4:32). The Lord had appeared to Solomon in a dream and said, "Ask for whatever you want Me to give you" (1 Kings 3:5). Solomon requested the gift of wisdom to govern his people and "to distinguish between right and wrong" (1 Kings 3:9). How abundantly God answered his petition! His forty-year reign was the golden age of prosperity for Israel, which never reached such heights before or since.

Solomon became the legendary paragon of wisdom. The "wisdom of Solomon" has itself become proverbial. He was a legend in his own time: "His fame spread to all the surrounding nations" (1 Kings 4:31). His wisdom and splendor entranced and won over the Queen of Sheba as recorded in one of the most captivating incidents in the Bible (1 Kings 10:1-10).

Solomon authored three books of the Bible. The Song of Solomon, the enchanting love song of the Bible, is believed to have been written when he was young. Proverbs was probably written during his middle age when his intellectual powers and kingdom were at their peak. Ecclesiastes seems to have been written in his waning years of disappointment and despair.

Many consider Solomon to be the wisest man who ever lived. From the ancient book of Proverbs we can tap his God-given wisdom and learn to live more wisely in the day-by-day business of life.

The English Romantic poet John Keats has given us a perceptive observation on proverbs: "Nothing ever becomes real till it is experienced. Even a proverb is no proverb to you till your life has illustrated it."[3] May our lives be illustrations of the truths we will encounter in this great Book of Proverbs.

> *Giver of every perfect gift, grant me a wise and understanding heart, a wisdom to discern between right and wrong.*

FOUR
A CALL TO EXCELLENCE

The fear of the Lord is the beginning of knowledge (1:7).

In Search of Excellence by Thomas Peters and Robert Waterman, Jr. became one of the top-selling and most discussed books in the early '80s. The book deals with excellence in business management and what makes organizations effective.

The instant success of the book reflected people's interest in the keys to excellence in the world of business. The authors acknowledge that their eight criteria for excellence are not often found in businesses — "as rare as a smog-free day in Los Angeles," they say. But when they are incorporated, success results.

God is interested in excellence. He does not want us to settle for mediocrity. He calls us to excellence in the moral realm. His will is that we be authentic and sterling in character and conduct.

That's what the Book of Proverbs is all about. It is a call, a challenge, a manual for excellence.

"The Proverbs," the title of the book, is derived from the opening phrase. The Hebrew word for proverbs, *mashal,* means "to be like," "to represent." It is an apt title since most proverbs use comparisons to teach their truths.

Proverbs are generalizations from experience. Their brevity, almost always under twenty-five words, makes them easy to remember.

"The proverbs of Solomon" reads the opening of this intriguing Bible book. We have already referred to the authorship of Proverbs, but "a word to the wise" is in order. Solomon allowed his riches and many wives to turn his heart away from the Lord. The latter part of his life was filled with the futility recorded in the Book of Ecclesiastes. We are reminded by the attribution to him at the very beginning of this book, that it is not enough to know what is right and wise. We must internalize and practice it.

The Living Bible vividly renders the book's statement of purpose: *He wrote them to teach his people how to live — how to act in every circumstance, for he wanted them to be understanding, just and fair in everything they did* (1:2-3).

"To know wisdom" (1:2, NASB) capsulizes this book's purpose. The Hebrew "to know" means more than satisfying intellectual curiosity, it involves experiencing the truth of the proverb. The wisdom of Proverbs is not mere head knowledge but divinely enlightened understanding of what is good and evil.

"The fear of the Lord is the beginning of knowledge" (1:7). "Reverence" is perhaps a more helpful translation than "fear." This verse could be a synopsis of the Book of Proverbs, and a good motto for life. "Fear of the Lord," like the four notes that present the theme of Beethoven's Fifth Symphony, appear at the beginning, as well as recurringly throughout the book. Its repetition underscores that fear or reverence for the Lord is the only foundation for wisdom. This preamble to God's book on wise living reminds us that true wisdom begins with a reverence for God.

> *God of wisdom, You have destined me for abundant living, for the heights; lead me beyond mediocrity to excellence.*

24

FIVE

WISDOM BEGINS AT HOME

Listen, my son, to your father's instruction and do not forsake your mother's teaching (1:8).

Home is the primary place for the transmission and learning of wisdom. God holds parents responsible for the moral education and training of their children. The father must fulfill the role of instructor, by both training and example. The mother is also a teacher. The Book of Proverbs has more to say about love and respect for mothers than any other Bible book.

Children grow up so fast. Before you know it the little girl in the frilly, feminine dress emerges as a woman in blue jeans. "As the twig is bent, so grows the tree." Parents must be faithful to their sacred responsibility for training children while they are still young. As the penman of Proverbs reminds us, enticements will beckon our youth to the paths of destruction.

Major cities today are plagued with crime and violence. Young people are entangled in the web of criminal activity and pay a heavy price. Often their lives are ruined. Our courts and prisons bear woeful witness to the epidemic of theft, robbery, drug abuse, violence, and murder.

The problem and seduction of crime is not new. Kenneth Taylor's *Living Bible* paraphrase of Proverbs advises a young man: "If young toughs tell you, 'Come and join us'—turn your back on them! 'We'll hide and rob and kill,' they say. . . . 'And the loot we'll get! All kinds of stuff! Come on, throw in your lot with us; we'll split with you in equal shares.' Don't do it, son! Stay far from men like that, for crime is their way of life, and murder is their specialty. . . . They lay a booby trap for their own lives. Such is the fate of all who live by violence and murder" (1:10-19).

Those who have worked in the trenches of human need and crisis have seen all too many living proofs of this portrait. A young man gets in with the wrong companions; they start to play fast and loose with the law, and the respect and rights of others are violated, often ending in tragedy. The tableau of crime next takes in the court scene and ends in the horrors of imprisonment.

Indeed, crime does not pay. It is inordinately costly for the person who becomes a criminal, and for the victims as well. "Such is the end of all who go after ill-gotten gain; it takes away the lives of those who get it" (1:19). The truth and warning of this text are as current as when written three millennia ago.

Christians have a responsibility to help prevent and reduce this evil in our crime-ridden and crime-terrorized society. We need to make our influence felt through legislation and education and ethics. Crime is a great evil that calls for our concern and involvement.

Just before William Jennings Bryan went off to college, he was summoned into his father's study. As he went in, he expected to receive a final sermon on the temptations of youth. But to his surprise, his father did not preach to him. Instead, he simply asked him if he would agree to read the Book of Proverbs through once a month for a year. William promised to do so, and throughout his freshman year he kept his word. Later in life, after he had become a respected statesman and a skillful orator, Bryan looked back at his father's request as one of the most influential factors in his life. Through his reading of Proverbs, he was given wisdom to overcome the pitfalls of that crucial year. If we help our youth build on the foundation of God's Word, they will be successful in the business of life.

A magazine ad for a family publication featured the book, *A Beautiful Baby,* and the words above the baby, "Yours. For a limited time only." Parents have so few years to teach and train their children in the all-important business of life. Let us faithfully impart the training, instruction, and example to lay the foundations for righteous living.

Heavenly Father, help me by example and precept to build, in young lives entrusted to me, foundations of true wisdom that will stand the tests of life's perils and pitfalls.

SIX

PREREQUISITES FOR WISDOM

Wisdom calls aloud in the street,
she raises her voice in the public squares (1:20-21).

Solomon personifies wisdom as a woman making an impassioned appeal. Her voice can be heard trying to break in upon us and enrich our lives with her largesse. Every time we open our Bible she speaks to us. When we commune with God in prayer, we hear her accents. When we see a godly life, we encounter her eloquence. When we worship, her whispered secrets fall upon our ears.

"Wisdom calls aloud." May we hear and heed her voice. She would speak to us at the busy crossroads of life — "in the squares . . . at the head of noisy streets . . . in the gateways of the city" (1:20-21).

Wisdom can be spurned: "You rejected me when I called and no one gave heed when I stretched out my hand . . . you ignored all my advice" (1:24-25). God has vouchsafed to give to each of us the privilege of free will. But the privilege also carries a solemn responsibility.

The consequences of rejecting the wisdom God offers are bitter. The words in the remainder of chapter 1 witness to the seriousness of such rejection: "Calamity overtakes you like a storm . . . disaster sweeps over you like a whirlwind . . . distress and trouble overwhelm you" (1:27).

28

The payday of sin, although sometimes delayed, will come. It metes out bitter wages. What a melancholy list of casualties is given of those who choose the foolish things of life over the wise ways of God.

If we are going to know God's wisdom, there are two prerequisites, presented as "if/then" statements.

The first prerequisite is a receptive spirit: "If you accept my words and store up my commands within you, turning your ear to wisdom and applying your heart to understanding" (2:1-2). It is not a passive but an active reception that is required. We need to "accept, store up, turn our ears, and apply our hearts."

The second prerequisite is a diligent seeking, as one calling out for it or a miner who digs deep into the earth in his search for it as for hidden treasure (see 2:3-4).

Do you want to discover the riches God has for you? Then you must pay the price. It is a hard-won treasure. It starts with a passionate longing for what God has for you. Then follows the hard work of "digging." You must go down into the mine shaft with your pick and axe. By the rugged, hard work of digging deep into God's Word and mining the riches of prayer, you will then discover the priceless treasures of God.

Such seeking and searching will adorn the life with the fruits of wisdom: knowledge of God (2:5-6), victory (2:7-8), discretion (2:9-15), moral safeguard from unchastity (2:16-19) and walking the path of the righteous (2:20-22).

Let's go down into the mine shaft!

Divine Wisdom, grant to me the diligence and discipline to search out the treasures of wisdom that will truly enrich my life.

SEVEN

DESTINED FOR GLORY

My son, do not forget my teaching,
but keep my commands in your heart (3:1).

"One of the golden words of religion is 'remember'," writes Charles Fritsch in *The Interpreter's Bible*. "There is no spiritual life or growth," he adds, "apart from the great spiritual heritage of the past."[4] Christian education must always go hand in hand with evangelism. A lack of teaching will result in stunted growth, mediocrity, and defeat.

The thoughtful reader may question the results of faithfulness promised by the proverbs: "For they will prolong your life many years and bring you prosperity" (3:2). Is the writer of Proverbs presenting a spurious health-and-wealth Gospel?

Does a life of faithful devotion assure a person many years? We quickly recall many whose lives were cut short because of their faithfulness. History abounds with the records of martyrs. Due to his faithful discipleship, Dietrich Bonhoeffer was executed at age thirty-nine on a gallows in a Nazi concentration camp. Jesus and most of His disciples suffered death early in life at the hands of the enemies of faith.

The Protestant Ethic aside, prosperity has never been considered a hallmark of Christian discipleship. Piety wedded to prosperity ends up being a bargain with God.

Too often in our day we have heard that we are saved to succeed and redeemed for riches. Secular mentality and materialism have infiltrated the church. A return to the teachings of Christ on the high cost of discipleship and the realities of living in a fallen world are prerequisites for modern-day discipleship.

Isolated from the deeper revelation of the New Testament, these proverbs would suggest that when a man dies young he was not a good man; if he suffers a reversal of fortune it must be due to blameworthy conduct; if he is prosperous it implies goodness.

There is, of course, an element of truth in that view which must not be ignored. Life often does go better when lived according to the principles of our faith. Power and productivity are evidenced in the total life when we live by the principles of the Bible. We need to interpret such Old Testament texts as this in the light of the life and teachings of Christ, the One who said, "I have come that they may have life, and have it to the full" (John 10:10, NIV). But the life to which Christ calls is one extravagant with spiritual riches of salvation, joy, purpose, peace, and power.

In this world we are called to the abundant life—Life with a capital L, life with zest, full of joy and peace, life that is purposeful and productive. And in the world to come, we're destined for glory.

Let us rise up and claim our inheritance!

God of grace and glory, grant to me Your wisdom from above, that I may rise up to my eternal destiny.

EIGHT

TRUST IN THE LORD

Trust in the Lord with all your heart (3:5).

What is there in life to which we can safely commit our trust? We cannot rely on ourselves; we are frail, fragile, finite. We cannot rely on nature. It is fickle—sometimes beautiful, sometimes savage and "red in tooth and claw." Others whom we trust may fail us. Organizations and governments betray their "feet of clay."

But the Lord is always faithful, dependable, immutable: "I the Lord do not change" (Mal. 3:6).

The royal sage of Proverbs directs us to the only and ultimate One to whom we can commit our lives. In the most memorable lines of his book, he sets forth the terms of what it means to live for God:

> Trust in the Lord with all your heart
>   and lean not on your own understanding;
> in all your ways acknowledge Him,
>   and He will make your paths straight (3:5-6).

It begins with the commitment of nothing less than "all your heart." There can be no reservations in our consecration. The trust of which the text speaks invokes all of life. It calls us to renounce our "own understanding," and in essence, to "bet our life" on God and His wisdom.

"Some may think such a directive proves God restrictive, narrow, dictatorial," writes Marlene Chase on this text. She perceptively adds, "But knowing us as perfectly as He does, God understands that this commandment is the only way of life that will result in our happiness."[5]

This beautiful and beloved text should be inscribed on the heart of every believer. Place it in the cupboard of memory, and bring it out often to savor its delectable nourishment for the soul.

The Greek mathematician Archimedes asked only for one fixed and immovable point in order to move the whole earth from its place—"so I may have great hopes if I find even the least thing that is unshakably certain." This proverb reveals that Archimedian point—the basis of all certainty—the Lord, Christ the Truth! He alone can sustain the whole structure of human knowledge and experience.

Let us acknowledge Him in all our ways and He will direct our paths. With the psalmist, we affirm, "In Thee do I put my trust" (Ps. 16:1, KJV). We dare not venture forth on the pilgrimage of life without a complete reliance on the presence of our Lord. Fanny Crosby has given devotional expression to this truth:

> I must have the Savior with me,
>   For I dare not walk alone;
> I must feel His presence near me,
>   And His arm around me thrown.
>
> I must have the Savior with me,
>   For my faith at best is weak;
> He can whisper words of comfort
>   That no other voice can speak.
>
> I must have the Savior with me
>   In the onward march of life;

Through the tempest and the sunshine,
Through the battle and the strife.

With His presence to guide and strengthen, we can make our way on life's pilgrimage with confidence and courage.

Heavenly Father, I trust You with all my heart and commit my life fully to Your love and leading.

NINE
STEWARDSHIP

Honor the Lord with your wealth,
with the firstfruits of all your crops (3:9).

We are not possessors but stewards of our wealth. We honor the Lord with the proper use of our material goods and by giving Him first claim on our possessions. The "firstfruits" belong to God, not that which is left over. The commitment of the Christian includes his money and possessions.

The virus of materialism infects our society today. "Things are in the saddle." We are caught up in a frenzied and futile ride toward a utopia where possessions are the ultimate quest. Today we face the danger of living under the tyranny of money and allowing our lives, values, and decisions to be dictated by money. Richard Foster, in *Money, Sex & Power*, calls us "to dethrone money,"[6] for it is too high on our list of values.

Money itself is not evil; it is our obsession and misuse of it that is wrong. Money is not "the root of all evil" as 1 Timothy 6:10 is often misquoted. Rather the text reads, "The love of money is the root of all kinds of evil." Our text in Proverbs calls us to a constructive use of wealth. We possess both the sacred duty and the high privilege to honor the Lord with our resources.

Tolstoy illustrates the peril of covetousness with a telling story in *How Much Land Does a Man Need?* A certain landowner in Russia offered his peasant, as a gift, as much land as he could encompass by walking from sunrise to sunset. The peasant started out traveling as fast as he could. Noon came and it was time to turn back. But he saw a beautiful meadow to the side of him and said, "I would like to have that in my possession." A little farther on he spied a fine wooded land and decided to take that in. On the other side a beautiful lake glistened and he said, "That ought to be mine also." Alas, when he rushed back to the starting place just as the sun was setting below the horizon, being pressed by greed, he dropped dead!

Emerson once said of money, "It costs too much." David Livingstone, who gave not only his substance but his whole life to Christ as missionary to Africa, wrote, "I will place no value on anything that I have or possess except in relation to the kingdom of Christ."

Gifts to God are never lost—they are investments in the bank of eternity, paying the highest dividends. John Bunyan expressed this truth in the couplet: "A man there was, and they called him mad; the more he gave, the more he had." What we give to God is all we will truly have in our account for eternity. Let's not forget to make deposits!

> *Heavenly Father, source of all our blessings and bounty, as a faithful steward help me invest my temporal resources in Your eternal kingdom.*

TEN

THE BLESSINGS OF BENEVOLENCE

Do not withhold good from those who deserve it,
when it is in your power to act (3:27).

We live in a society with great disparities and inequities between rich and poor. We live in a world where millions suffer the ravages of absolute poverty and the scourge of malnutrition and death from droughts. This text in Proverbs has never been more up to date: "Do not withhold good from those who deserve it, when it is in your power to act. Do not say to your neighbor, 'Come back later; I will give it tomorrow'—when you now have it with you" (3:27-28).

God holds us accountable for helping others in need. Jesus dramatically underscored this truth in His graphic depiction of the final judgment and the criterion for admission into the eternal kingdom of God: "For I was hungry and you gave Me food; I was thirsty and you gave Me drink; I was a stranger and you took Me in; I was naked and you clothed Me; I was sick and you visited Me; I was in prison and you came to Me" (Matt. 25:35-36, NKJV).

The spiritual sensation of the believer should not be "How much must I give?" but rather "How much can I give?" A stingy Christian is as contradictory as dry rain, salty sugar, silent music, or dark sunshine.

Our text breaks the rainbow of benevolence into its elements of splendor. First we are to provide *good* for the deserving when we have the power to do so. There are many good things we can do when we have resources. We can help with education, enrichment opportunities, spiritual training, health progress, and other forms of aid that bring good to those who deserve our action. We can spread a rainbow of hope amid the storms that enter the lives of others.

Our benevolence needs to be *selective* — "those who deserve it." There should be a discernment in our giving. We must take time to evaluate the needs and the channels to meet those needs. Unfortunately, some funding appeals for charity have lacked integrity or proper accountability. The use of our resources for the good of others is vital. We need to ensure that "the deserving" will be the beneficiaries and that we identify the priorities of need as well as people.

Doing good is described as a *power.* Imagine having the power to satisfy and nourish a hungry person! The power to save lives from death by famine! The power to educate a young person! The power to cheer a needy family at Christmas! The power to bring healing from disease! Our resources, when motivated by God's love, become a power to do good.

Our text emphasizes the *timing* of our benevolence. It should be spontaneous, uncalculated, overflowing from a sensitive and generous spirit. We are told not to do it "tomorrow" but "now." Another proverb outside the Bible says, "He gives twice who gives promptly." Giving without reluctance or waiting bestows added blessing.

Let us beware the epidemic of materialism in our society. The teaching of this text offers an effective antidote.

> *Loving God, make me a cup of strength and solace to those who suffer, and help me live simply in our hungry and hurting world.*

ELEVEN
IN MY FATHER'S HOUSE

The Lord's curse is on the house of the wicked,
but he blesses the home of the righteous (3:33).

In Proverbs the family holds the pivotal place in society. This book of Scripture portrays the family as the fundamental unit of the nation, as a cohesive bond of relationships. Husband, wife, parent, and children relationships receive constructive attention from this book of practical religion. What, after all, is more practical than family life?

In our day of unprecedented breakdown in the family, we would do well to heed the wisdom found in these pages. Our text offers one of the beautiful beatitudes of Proverbs: "He blesses the home of the righteous" (3:33).

What is there nearer heaven than a family and home blessed by the presence and spirit of Christ in its midst? The words of Arthur Arnott express it well:

> Home is home, however lowly,
> Home is sweet when love is there,
> Home is home when hearts are holy,
> Earth has ne'er a spot so fair.
> Jesus makes our home a heaven,
> Sacred in the fireside warm;
> After battling through the long day,
> Home's a shelter from the storm.[7]

39

Solomon pays a moving tribute to his mother, Bathsheba, and his father, David, who trained him in the ways of God from his most tender years. "When I was a boy in my father's house," he says, "still tender, and an only child of my mother, he taught me and said, 'Lay hold of my words with all your heart; keep my commands and you will live' " (4:3-4).

Three generations are represented in this heritage of religious training. Solomon, who had received it from his parents, now passes it on to his children. The blessings of Christian family are passed from generation to generation. Devout parents can never estimate the longevity of their influence for God upon succeeding generations.

Four scholars were said to argue over Bible translations. One said he preferred the *King James Version* because of its stately and eloquent old English. Another said he preferred the *New American Standard Bible* for its accuracy, and a third, the Moffatt translation because of its penetrating use of words. The fourth scholar admitted, "I personally prefer my mother's translation. She translated each page into life. It's the most convincing translation I ever saw."

Family cycles are all too well known by sociologists who have researched the intergenerational patterns of families. They have documented that abused children are more apt to become abusing parents, alcoholics tend to rear offspring who become alcoholics, children of broken families have a higher incidence of divorce, and so on. But the good news of our text is that the modeling of God's will and wisdom also has a chain effect for future generations. What an awesome thought—that what we are and do before our children may have an impact upon our great great grandchildren whom we will never know! The sacred responsibility of parenting requires that it be handled with prayer.

Ancient Israel believed religion should be taught as well as caught. Precept and practice went hand in hand.

There is no better place to give religious instruction than in the home and no better time than early in life. To be brought up "in the nurture and admonition of the Lord" (Eph. 6:4, KJV) is a blessing beyond compare. No greater legacy can be passed on to our children, nothing will more enhance and enrich their lives.

Father, for the joy of human love, we thank You. Be the unseen Guest in our home. Help us to love, care for, and affirm those near and dear to us.

TWELVE
BIBLICAL ILLITERACY

Lay hold of my words with all your heart;
keep my commands and you will live (4:4).

The three R's, *readin', 'ritin', and 'rithmetic,* have stood the tests of time as the gateways to education and knowledge. *Readin'* especially is a foundation of learning. The wisdom of the ages is stored in the libraries of the world.

The acceleration of technology has created a global village which more than ever imposes the need to keep up with the times. The story is told that on the night the astronauts first neared the moon for a landing, a Nova Scotian farmer looked up and, seeing a thin crescent moon in the sky, commented, "You'd think they'd wait at least till it was bigger than that!" Our quest for knowledge is hard pressed to keep up with the fast-forward events of our day.

Yet a vast number of people in the world cannot read. Illiteracy looms as one of the great concerns of our time. It disenfranchises people from essential information and enrichment that comes from reading. Illiteracy spawns social and intellectual poverty. To be without the wealth of information and inspiration from the literary treasures is to be poor indeed. Man's literary legacy offers accumulated knowledge to apply to our contemporary world. As the famed physicist Sir Isaac Newton said, "I could see far because I stood on the shoulders of giants."

Today's video cult has struck what some consider a mortal blow to the art of reading. Video permeates every corner of our culture and has become our teacher, seller, entertainer. We have witnessed the miniaturization of the universe by computer, satellites, and worldwide television. Anthropologists may someday look back on this age as the period of an evolutionary jump to Video Man. Books, many predict, will be out of style and, like the typewriter, will yield to the new technology.

But there is one book that must never become outdated or obsolete. The Word of God is eternal. Mankind will need its guidance and inspiration as long as he inhabits this sin-stained planet. In his book *Helps to Holiness,* Samuel Brengle called the Bible "God's recipe book for making holy people, God's guide book to show men and women the way to heaven, God's doctor book to show people how to get rid of soul-sickness."[8]

The most tragic illiteracy of all is biblical illiteracy. To not read or know its wisdom and to miss out on its fabulous wealth is to be poor indeed. Our text states that we are to "lay hold" of those words that enable us to truly live.

Biblical illiteracy is often voluntary, the product of neglect. It takes commitment and time to read and know the Bible. It is not to be read as any other book. It requires meditation, digestion, assimilation, and then expression in life. Its timeless texts need to be committed to memory, for memory is the sheath in which the sword of the Lord is kept. Then, knowing its truths and commands, we will be able to lay hold on eternal life.

Popular conference speaker Howard Hendricks is credited with defining three stages of Bible study. First there is the "castor oil" stage—when you study the Bible because you know it's good for you, but you don't find it enjoyable. Next there is "cereal" stage—your Bible reading gives you nourishment, but you find it somewhat dry and uninteresting. Finally, there is the "peaches-and-cream" stage when you discover the delectability of God's Word and enjoy studying it. With a change of metaphor, let us say with the psalmist that the Word of God to us is "sweeter than honey, than honey from the comb" (Ps. 19:10).

Dwight L. Moody's guidelines for the Bible still apply: "*Admit* it to be God's Word. *Submit* to its truths. *Commit* much of it to memory. *Transmit* it to others."

If you have not already done so, make a commitment now to daily reading and meditation of God's Word. Memorize at least one verse a day. Imagine how enriched life would become with the deposit of more than 300 verses a year in the vault of your mind and soul! The dividends would be fantastic!

Lord, with the psalmist I would pray, "Open my eyes that I may see wonderful things in Your law" (Ps. 119:18).

THIRTEEN
THE SHINING LIGHT

The path of the righteous is like
the first gleam of dawn,
shining ever brighter till
the full light of day (4:18).

The *King James Version* rendering of Proverbs 4:18 is justly famous:

> But the path of the just is as the shining light,
> that shineth more and more unto the perfect day.

The pilgrim on the Christian way discovers increasing brightness on his path. His ever closer walk with his Lord floods his way with the radiance of the Light of the World. He seeks the new city where night shall be no more, "for the glory of God gives it light, and the Lamb is its lamp" (Rev. 21:23).

John Bunyan's classic allegory, *Pilgrim's Progress*, illustrates this truth for us. He writes:

> The man . . . looking upon Evangelist very carefully, said, "Whither must I fly?"
> Then said Evangelist, pointing with his finger over a very wide field, "Do you see yonder wicket gate?"
> The man said, "No."
> Then said the other, "Do you see yonder shining light?"

He said, "I think I do."

Then said Evangelist, "Keep that light in your eye, and go up directly thereto, so shalt thou see the gate; at which, when thou knockest, it shall be told thee what thou shalt do."

The Christian on his pilgrimage constantly follows the One who is the Light of the World. The pilgrim also is guided by the light of the Word and the indwelling presence of the Holy Spirit. There is a "yonder light" that illumines and brightens our pathway when we follow the leading of our Lord.

The path of the Christian, as our text reveals, glows with increasing brightness as we journey on in our pilgrimage. Our faith becomes stronger, our understanding of God's truths clearer, our experience with God more intimate. This radiant truth has been expressed in some of our old hymns that testify, "Further on, the way grows brighter," and "My way has brighter grown / Since I've learned to trust Him more."

The Christian pathway is filled with joyful expectation and shining serendipities.

> *Lead, kindly Light, amid the encircling gloom,*
> *Lead Thou me on!*
> *The night is dark, and I am far from home;*
> *Lead Thou me on!*
> *Keep Thou my feet; I do not ask to see*
> *The distant scene—one step enough for me.*
> *—John Henry Newman*

FOURTEEN
GUARDING THE HEART

Above all else, guard your heart (4:23).

The heart figures prominently in this book of practical wisdom for the Christian life. It appears nearly 100 times in Proverbs. It is used as a synonym for the whole inner being. It is the seat and source of the inner man. It embraces his emotions, affections, motives, will, intellect.

We need "above all else" to *guard* our hearts. This strong word *guard* indicates there are dangers and enemies of the heart. Diligence is required to protect our hearts from the perils that can overtake them.

The Book of Proverbs elsewhere identifies some of the types of "heart trouble": a wicked heart (6:18), sensual heart (7:25), deceitful heart (12:20), anxious heart (12:25), bitter heart (14:10), aching heart (14:13), proud heart (18:12), raging heart (19:3), and envious heart (23:17).

The key to health is a healthy heart. The heart is described as "the wellspring of life." It is the hidden fountain source from which all conduct springs forth into the outer life. If the source is pure, then the outcome will be pure. But if the source is impure, then it will flaw the character and conduct of the life that emanates from it.

What do we allow in our heart? Do we guard it diligently? With prayer? With the Word? With worship? With association of God's people? With loving obedience to our Lord? This proverb, "Above all else, guard your heart," contains the very key of life and eternity for each of us.

The story is told of a young man who was the son of a famous surgeon, and who played first base for his college team. One day a slight mischance left his index finger badly swollen and lame. That night his physician father noticed him shielding it as he ate dinner. After the meal he took the young man aside for a careful examination of the injury. When he had assured himself that no permanent damage had been done, he turned to his son and said, "You have told me that you want to be a surgeon. You may have to choose between surgery and baseball. Wouldn't it be tragic if twenty years from now, a little child would die on the operating table under your hands because that finger was too stiff to allow you to perform the operation with speed and skill?"

The next day, after careful reflection on the goals and priorities of his life, the young man turned in his glove and uniform. "I'm going to be a surgeon," he said to the coach, "and I don't intend to let anything interfere with that purpose for my life." He had learned to unify his life under its priorities and purpose.

Following Christ demands guarding the heart. It's the best practice for assuring our spiritual health and happiness.

> *"Search me, O God, and know my heart. . . .*
> *See if there is any offensive way in me,*
> *and lead me in the way everlasting" (Ps. 139:23-24).*

FIFTEEN

THE HIGH COST OF SEXUAL SIN

Her [adulteress] feet go down to death (5:5).

The Book of Proverbs devotes more space to the subject of sexual relations than to any other. God must be vitally interested in our leading pure sex lives.

Sex too often has been allowed to turn to license and lust. "Many are the victims . . . brought down" by lust and "her slain are many" (7:26). Perhaps the writer was thinking of the lust that ruined Samson or slew David! We can all too painfully call to mind strong men who have fallen victim to sexual sin.

The social convention of that time accounts for these sections addressed to "my son." It was the age of male supremacy; only men were given the benefit of religious instruction (which is the basis of Isaac Bashevis Singer's short story plot, Yentl). The contemporary application of these verses, however, is to daughters as well as sons on the subject of sexual relations.

The sage of Proverbs writes of the seductress and the allurements of sin (5:1-6). He graphically portrays sin's enticements. But there is always an afterward, and Proverbs does not allow us to forget it. "But in the end" (5:4), warns the text. Nothing can be judged by its beginning. What starts out delicious ends up disgusting.

The drama is even more vividly portrayed in chapter 7, verses 6-27. The setting is the harlot's house, at twilight. The victim, a young man "who lacked judgment," wanders the street. The "huntress," "dressed to kill," cleverly seduces the young man with her flattery and sensuous appeal as she entices, "Come, let's drink deep of love . . . let's enjoy ourselves with love!" (7:18)

Then follows "the kill" as the young man yields and becomes "like an ox going to the slaughter, like a deer stepping into a noose . . . like a bird darting into a snare, little knowing it will cost him his life" (7:22-23). Sexual immorality seems to anesthetize the judgment. Appropriately, this major warning against sexual promiscuity closes with the word *death* (7:27).

A moment of pleasure in sin always exacts too high a price. "The flesh and thy body are consumed" (5:11, KJV) depicts some physical dangers of promiscuity. Dissolute living often produces disease. A feature in a 1990 *Newsweek* reported: "The United States is currently in the grip of an STD (sexually transmitted diseases) outbreak of unprecedented proportions. The statistics are awesome: one in four Americans between the ages of fifteen and fifty-five will acquire STD at some point in his or her life. Twenty-seven thousand cases are contracted every day." And the further epidemic of AIDS is the most alarming consequence of all.

The wise counsel of this teaching of Proverbs is timely. Someone has said that if God approved of the permissiveness of our society, He would have given us "The Ten Suggestions" instead of "The Ten Commandments." The ancient Book of Proverbs calls us back to God's standard of purity.

> *Holy Spirit, help me make sex the servant of Your holy purpose. Create in me a clean heart and a pure mind that will enable me to live above the permissive style of the world around me.*

SIXTEEN

INTIMACY IN MARRIAGE

Rejoice in the wife of your youth (5:18).

Proverbs does not espouse an ascetic concept of sex. After condemning sexual promiscuity, the writer presents a beautiful plea for love in the marriage relationship. Extramarital relations are contrary to God's will, but sexual fulfillment in marriage has divine approval.

To his sons, the writer urges them to "rejoice in the wife of your youth" (5:18). He advises to take water "from your own cistern" and "from your own well," meaning for a man to have sexual intercourse only with his wife.

Intimacy in marriage is God's will. In erotic language similar to that found in the Song of Solomon, Proverbs makes it clear that God has ordained sexual delight within the marriage bond (5:15-20).

We desperately need this message in this day of disposable marriages, living-together arrangements, homosexual marriages, and open marriages. We must once more reaffirm marriage as God's sacred ordinance.

True, marital land is not Disneyland. It possesses struggles, sufferings, setbacks. It requires an unflagging commitment. It calls for acceptance, which in marriage is the power to love someone even when he or she falls short of our hopes.

God designed marriage for intimacy. He planned that "they shall become one flesh" (Mark 10:8). God ordained marriage to transcend romantic love, to become a lifetime union and partnership that is mutually fulfilling. Marriage in the will of God is commitment that learns to adjust, accept, and affirm each other in a lifelong process of growing.

"Rejoice in the wife of your youth" is the up-to-date counsel from this age-old book. Fellow husbands, make a list of thirty qualities you appreciate about your wife and for the next month, tell her one of them each day. It may put some zip in that marriage and turn a bland relationship into a bright union.

Lord, who by Your presence blessed the marriage at Cana in Galilee, help me keep my marriage vows inviolate, to deal tenderly with my mate's dreams, realizing that no other human ties are more tender, no other vows more sacred than those which blend two lives into one.

SEVENTEEN

MONEY MATTERS

My son, if you have put up security for your neighbor
. . . if you have been trapped by what you said (6:1-2).

The "bottom line" of this text is the principle of prudence to avoid committing ourselves beyond limits of our resources. It calls to a wise handling of our money.

Does this text have something to say to our "buy-now-pay-later" syndrome? How many people today are done in by their plastic credit cards? They are "ensnared, trapped" by spending beyond their means, buying frills rather than planning and investing wisely. The lure of deferred payment for instant satisfaction takes precedence over wise management in money matters.

Socrates, who saw the world with a humorous and philosophical eye, reportedly said, "Bless me," looking around the marketplace with its profusion of all an Athenian could want, "what a lot of things there are a man can do without." Too often we consider necessary something not only could we do quite well without, but might even do better without. "Compulsive extravagance is a modern mania," writes Richard Foster in *Money, Sex & Power.* "The contemporary lust for 'more, more, more' is clearly psychotic; it has lost touch with reality."[9]

John Wesley once said that Christians should "gain all they can, save all they can, and give all they can." This philosophy and practice would be endorsed by the writer of Proverbs who advocates frugality and discretion in money matters.

Our proverb for this chapter warns us that we can be "trapped" by grasping for more than we should. A telling example of that peril is the story of the European wrestling champ, Yussif, the Terrible Turk. Yussif was not satisfied with all the glory and money he had won in Europe. He challenged the American wrestling champion, Strangler Lewis. The 350-pound Turk won the world championship match and demanded his winning purse be paid in U.S. gold. He did not trust anyone else to hold his gold but crammed it into the money belt he wore around his huge circumference. Many miles at sea, the ship S.S. Burgoyne, on which he sailed back to Europe, began to sink. Yussif would not part with his gold and went over the side of the boat with his bulging belt still strapped to his frame. Before lifeboats could reach him, he plunged to the bottom of the Atlantic.

Jesus spoke more about money matters than any other subject, warning against materialism. Possessions tend to dominate our lives. They can make us lose sight of life's priorities. The wise management of our money is one of life's sacred responsibilities.

Martin Luther reminds us that three conversions are necessary: the conversion of the heart, mind, and purse.

Christ, who gave the sublime example of simplicity, curb my material desires and help me not to sacrifice the eternal for the temporal, the treasures for the tinsel of this life.

EIGHTEEN
CONSIDER THE ANT

Go to the ant, you sluggard;
consider its ways and be wise! (6:6).

An anthill is a busy place. Every member of the colony has its job to do. Benjamin Franklin's Poor Richard alluded to the ant's industry when he said, "None preaches better than the ant, and she says nothing." Mentioned only twice in the Bible, here and in 30:25, the ant does preach a powerful sermon on industry.

The next time this pesky invertebrate invades your picnic, consider the marvels of this insect that Edward O. Wilson, the leading expert on ants, says "rules the world." Entomologists tell us that the ant is the most dominant social insect; there are 8,800 known species, and ants exist almost everywhere except in the polar regions. They constitute over 10 percent of the world's animal biomass, the total weight of all fauna. They turn most of the world's soil, aerate, drain, and enrich it, and as scavengers eat more than 90 percent of the corpses of small animals. Without its prodigious work, hundreds of thousands of plant and animal species would become extinct and the world's ecosystem destabilized. The ant is a walking chemical factory, equipped with a sophisticated communications system and weaponry. Its life has no meaning apart from its prodigious work with its coded instinct to harvest for the winter and to work for the good and survival of the colony. The poet teacher of Proverbs could not begin to realize the profound truth he wrote when he cited the lowly ant as an example of diligence. Its complex industry is without peer in the fauna of the world.

Indolence is a terrible weakness and is inconsistent with the Christian life. There is work for all to do. Each must carry his own load. The indolent and the sluggard become parasites, living off the labor of others. A good motto of the past was, "An honest day's pay for an honest day's work." Our Scripture text speaks to us of the importance of industry over laziness.

The threefold repetition of "little" underscores how minor neglects can result in major deficiencies: "A little sleep, a little slumber, a little folding of the hands to rest—and poverty will come on you like a bandit" (6:10-11).

We are reminded of Jesus' words: "He who is faithful in what is least is faithful also in much" (Luke 16:10, NKJV). The little duties, the details that make a difference, often separate expedience from excellence.

Jesus sanctified human toil working in the carpenter shop for the better part of His life. Then, shaking the wood shavings from His tunic for the last time, He said, "I must do the work of Him who sent me." He spent Himself in toil for the accomplishment of His sacred task.

Leslie Taylor Hunt, in his lyric, reminds us of our our work's ultimate purpose:

> All my best works are naught,
>   Please they not Thee;
> Far past my busy hands
>   Thine eye doth see
> Into the depths of mind,
>   Searching the plan designed,
> Gladdened when Thou dost find
>   First of all, Thee.[10]

Our work, when done to please God, becomes not a drag but a delight, not a burden but a blessing, not a frustration but a fulfillment. How deprived we would be if life were all leisure with no opportunity to be productive and contributive to our community and others.

Antonio Stradivari distinguished himself as the world's greatest violin maker. His instruments were unsurpassed. Modern violin makers have been unable to equal the instruments of the old Italian masters of the seventeenth and eighteenth centuries. Stradivari once remarked, "If my hand slacked, I should rob God." That is a good motto for every person. God has given talents and gifts to each of us and we are responsible, not only to men, but to God for how we use them.

Christ, who toiled at the carpenter's bench, give me mind, heart, and hands to do Your will and work. Help me as a faithful steward to help build Your kingdom here on earth.

NINETEEN

PORTRAIT OF DIVINE WISDOM

Does not wisdom call out? (8:1)

Chapter 8 opens in the bustle of life and proceeds to soar beyond time and space. Wisdom personified heralds the good tidings, not in the halls of learning but in the open air; not in the precincts of the temple but in the market-place, in the most public and conspicuous places. The message resounds: God is as relevant as the busy commerce of our daily lives.

Unlike the harlot of our previous chapter, wisdom's voice sounds strong and clear. There is no whispering, no subtle hints of secret pleasures. She is open, straightforward, honest, pure.

Her invitation is universal—"I raise my voice to all mankind" (8:4). Her rewards give strong incentive for heeding her invitation (8:18-21, 35-36; 9:11-12).

This magnificent Scripture anticipates New Testament teachings on Christ found in John 1:1-14, 1 Corinthians 1:24, 30; Colossians 1:15-18; Hebrews 1:1-4. In this portrait of Christ as Wisdom Incarnate, His eternal and preincarnate existence are recorded in immortal words. The poet penman of Proverbs transcends his time, reaching back into eternity to present this inspired portrait of Christ as the Craftsman of Creation.

The Lord possessed me at the beginning of His work,
  before His deeds of old;
I was appointed from eternity,
  from the beginning, before the world began.
When there were no oceans, I was given birth,
  when there were no springs abounding with water;
before the mountains were settled in place,
  before the hills, I was given birth,
before He made the earth or its fields
  or any of the dust of the world (8:22-26).

His delight in mankind is also portrayed:

I was filled with delight day after day,
  rejoicing always in His presence,
rejoicing in His whole world
  and delighting in mankind (8:30-31).

Some have called this "the greatest passage in the Book of Proverbs." It depicts Divine Wisdom manifest in creation.

Many Bible scholars interpret this text as a prophetical portrait of Christ. It has been termed by Charles Fritch as "one of the most perfect pictures of Christ to be found in the Old Testament . . . a portraiture of the essential wisdom of God personified, the Logos of later books and the Gospel."[11]

Athanasius, an early church leader, wielded this text in one of the great doctrinal crises on the divinity of Christ. The Nicene creed draws its Christology from the deep well of this text.

This sublime portrait of Christ as the Wisdom of God reminds us that our Lord is the summit of all knowledge, the goal of all goodness, the crown of all character, the perfection of all beauty, the inspiration of all hope, the illustration of all truth, and the manifestation of all might. He transcends all our creeds and structures. The crown of divinity rests upon His brow. The scepter of universal dominion clings to His hand. O come, let us adore Him — Christ the Lord!

Christ, who became Wisdom Incarnate, help me hear and heed Your voice that calls me to ultimate knowledge and truth.

TWENTY

THE DIVINE CRAFTSMAN

I was there when He set the heavens in place. . . .
Then I was the craftsman at His side (8:27, 30).

It staggers the imagination to ponder this portrait of Christ as the Divine Craftsman of Creation. What stupendous power, what awesome wisdom, what eternal ages are capsulized in this sublime and stirring depiction from the inspired sage some 3,000 years ago.

I was there when He set the heavens in place,
  when He marked out the horizon on the face of
  the deep,
when He established the clouds above
  and fixed securely the fountains of the deep,
when He gave the sea its boundary
  so the waters would not overstep His command,
and when He marked out the foundations of the
  earth.
Then I was the craftsman at His side (8:27-30).

What infinite depths of time, wisdom and power are intrinsic to the statement attributed to the preincarnate Christ, when God created the cosmos: "Then I was the craftsman at His side." In his magnificent prologue, John in his Gospel articulates the same theme of the eternal

Logos, Christ the wisdom of God, the divine agent of Creation: "Through Him all things were made; without Him nothing was made that has been made" (1:3). The Apostle Paul proclaims the same sublime truth: "For by Him all things were created: things in heaven and on earth, visible and invisible, whether thrones or powers or rulers or authorities; all things were created by Him and for Him" (Col. 1:16).

We often meditate upon the miracle of Christ's incarnation, the majesty of His teachings, the marvel of His miracles, and the might of His atonement. But we sometimes miss the majesty and magnificence of the preincarnate Christ—the Sovereign of eternal existence, of infinite wisdom and power.

Quoting from my book *100 Portraits of Christ:* "He created not only the macroscopic with its fiery planets and its unimaginable reaches of intergalactic space, but He created the microscopic as well. He polished the eye of every tiny insect, painted the bell of the lily, and crafted the exquisite geometry of the snowflake. He is the One who has made 'all things bright and beautiful, all creatures great and small.' "[12]

Quoting again from that same chapter on Christ as *The Mighty God:* "Before He ever came to earth, His hands tumbled solar systems and galaxies into space. He set the stars on their courses. He kindled the fires of the sun. He scooped out the giant beds of our mighty oceans" (p. 21).

> His holy fingers formed the bough
> Where grew the thorns that crowned His brow.
> The nails that pierced the hands were mined
> In secret places He designed.
>
> He made the forests whence there sprung
> The tree on which His holy body hung.
> He died upon a cross of wood
> Yet made the hill upon which it stood.

The sun which hid from Him its face
By His decree was poised in space.
The sky which darkened o'er His head
By Him above the earth was spread.

The spear that spilt His precious blood
Was tempered in the fires of God.
The grave in which His form was laid
Was hewn in rocks His hands had made.
—F.W. Pitt

There are many peaks of towering truth in the Book of Proverbs. But this eighth chapter rises in lofty grandeur as a Matterhorn to pierce the very heights of the heavens and eternity. It opens a window on a rare glimpse of the ineffable splendor and inexpressible majesty of the Sovereign Christ.

God, who paints the wayside flower and lights the evening stars, thank You for the revelation of Your love as well as Your power in the universe.

TWENTY-ONE

FEAST OR FOLLY

> *Wisdom ... calls from the highest point of the city (9:1, 3).*

Two crucial invitations are given to each new generation. Every individual must choose between them. The destiny for life and eternity hangs in the balance. One is the invitation to the banquet of life, the other to death.

Wisdom is personified as a gracious hostess. She has "built her house ... she has also set her table ... and she calls ... 'Come, eat my food ... walk in the way of understanding' " (9:1-6).

In contrast to the banquet of life to which Wisdom invites us is the invitation to the feast of Folly. Unlike her gracious rival, "the woman Folly is loud; she is undisciplined and without knowledge" (9:13). Her menu consists of "stolen water" and her clandestine banquet hall is filled with her victims. "But little do they know that the dead are there, "that her guests are in the depths of the grave" (9:18).

The invitations of Wisdom and Folly present the necessity of choice. Robert Browning in his poem "The Ring and the Book" has put it well — "life's business being just the terrible choice."[13] For each of us there is the burden of choice between wisdom and folly, good and evil, God and Satan, life and death.

James Russell Lowell expressed it memorably over a century ago:

> Once to every man and nation comes the moment
> to decide;
> In the strife of Truth and Falsehood,
> for the good or evil side.[14]

Wisdom is equated with knowledge of God as Proverbs repeats its profound truth: "The fear of the Lord is the beginning of wisdom." In this instance, however, the writer amplifies the proclamation: "and knowledge of the Holy One is understanding" (9:10). John Milton, peerless poet of the seventeenth century, gives a consummate summation: "The end of all learning is to know God and out of that knowledge to love and serve Him."

Legend tells of the beautiful Helen of Troy, over whom many battles were fought. When the army returned to Greece, after one of the battles, Helen was not on any of the ships. Menelaus went to try to find her, at great personal peril. He finally found her in a seaport village. She had been suffering from amnesia. Forgetting who she was, she was living as a prostitute.

Menelaus found her in rags, dirt, shame, and dishonor. He looked at her and called, "Helen." Her head turned. "You are Helen of Troy!" he said. And with those words, her back straightened and the royal look came back. She remembered who she was. She recalled her destiny.

We are destined to be children of the King. When we respond to God's invitation, we rise up to our noble heritage and the honor God has chosen for us. God's call is to greatness, to immortality, to our eternal destiny. Let us ever turn aside from the enticements of Folly and heed God's call, which leads us in the way of Wisdom.

Christ the Way, who calls to us, "Follow Me," give me wisdom and grace to follow where You lead.

65

TWENTY-TWO
MAXIMS AND MEMORIES

A wise son brings joy to his father,
but a foolish son grief to his mother (10:1).

We now leave the lengthy discourses of the first nine chapters and enter the second division of Proverbs (10:1–22:16) which consists of 375 two-line couplets ascribed to Solomon. Each one-verse aphorism is an entity in itself. This collection of miscellaneous maxims lacks any logical arrangement. These proverbs are written in poetic style, with three major types of poetic parallelism as hallmarks of the Book of Proverbs. Our text is an example of *antithetic parallelism* which contrasts in the second the truth of the first line.

Synonymous parallelism has the second line restate in a slightly different way the truth of the first line, so as to reinforce its meaning:

Pride goes before destruction,
a haughty spirit before a fall (16:18).

Synthetic parallelism advances in the second line the thought of the first:

In the way of righteousness there is life;
along that path is immortality (12:28).

The contrasting couplets are dominant through chapter 15 and are characterized by the key word *but*. The largely parallel forms from 16:3 through 22:16 feature the key word *and*. R.L. Harris, in his commentary on Proverbs, reminds us "that this is not a *Poor Richard's Almanac* of pithy, common sense sayings bearing on life's problems; this is a divine collection of sayings pointing out the way of holiness."[15]

The penman of Proverbs affirms: "A wise son brings joy to his father, but a foolish son grief to his mother" (10:1). As every parent knows, children can bring joy or crushing heartache. Love is a vulnerable thing. C.S. Lewis writes of the risks that accompany the rewards of love, but he reminds us that "hell is the only place outside heaven where we can be safe from the dangers of love."[16]

Throughout Proverbs, the mark of wisdom is filial regard on the part of the young man. The honoring of father and mother ranks high on the list of values. Children need to be careful that they bring joy and not grief to their parents. The poignant cry of David, "O Absalom, my son, my son," too often is echoed from a modern parent's heart for a loved son or daughter who has gone astray. The cords of love are tender and all too intricately twined around the hearts of others.

Solomon also identifies the two options for every life: "The memory of the righteous will be a blessing, but the name of the wicked will rot" (10:7). How will people remember us when we have departed the stage of life? Someday all that will be left of our lives and work will be memories. What will those memories be?

The benediction of a godly life will linger as fragrant evergreens in the garden of memory.

> *Lord, help me so live as to leave the legacy of a memory of blessing to those whom I have known and loved.*

67

TWENTY-THREE

"WINKING AT SIN"

Winking at sin leads to sorrow (10:10, TLB).

History abounds with lessons that illustrate this text. The Christian church has often been slow to recognize that "winking at sin," or silence in the face of evil, has been one of Satan's best weapons. The evils of society flourish in the fertile atmosphere of complacency and silence.

The question always haunts us, "How far should the Christian and the church be involved in politics?" Perhaps a rephrasing of the question helps clarify the issue: "Should politicians be left to make crucial moral decisions without constructive criticism from concerned Christians?" The answer must, of course, be an unequivocal, "No." It is not simply permissible for Christians to speak out. It is their God-appointed duty. The Gospel calls us to resist evil in all its forms.

Christians must not wink at the evils of abortion, alcohol and drugs, drunk driving, euthanasia, gambling, homosexuality, pornography, racism, sexual permissiveness, commercialization of the Sabbath, the poisoning of our environment. Christians in America should declare all-out war on such moral cancers as drugs and pornography, the latter fueling sex-related crimes and child sexual abuse, which plague our society today.

When Adolph Hitler was instituting his programs against the Jewish minority and appointing his Reich's bishops into leadership, many said "the church ought to keep its nose out of politics." It did. And this statement became its excuse for accommodation to protect its own interests. But a few—men like Dietrich Bonhoeffer and Martin Neimoller—saw through the fog and knew that religion had a great deal to do with politics when politics were evil and inhumanly cruel. Neimoller, who resisted the evils of Hitler and paid the price of seven years in the concentration camp, barely escaping execution, was later to write:

> In Germany they came first for the Communists, and I didn't speak up because I wasn't a Communist. Then they came for the Jews, and I didn't speak up because I wasn't a Jew. Then they came for the trade unionists, and I didn't speak up because I wasn't a trade unionist. Then they came for the Catholics, and I didn't speak up because I was a Protestant. Then they came for me, and by that time no one was left to speak up.[17]

In all realms of life, sin and evil must be taken with dead seriousness. To wink at sin is to court disaster.

For the Christian, there can be no cease-fires in the war against evil. God enlists believers to "put on the full armor of God so that you can take your stand against the devil's schemes" (Eph. 6:10).

Righteous God, grant me the indignations of Jesus Christ.

TWENTY-FOUR

DARE TO DISCIPLINE

*He who heeds discipline shows the way to life
(10:17).*

The words *discipline* and *disciple* are closely related. One
cannot be a disciple without discipline. Discipline is characterized by self-control, orderliness, efficiency, self-mastery. These qualities are hallmarks of the Christian life.

Our text states that the one who heeds discipline becomes an example of the way to live. Richard Foster
commences his classic devotional book, *Celebration of
Discipline,* with the statement, "Superficiality is the curse
of our age." The classical disciplines, he writes, "call us
to move beyond surface living into the depths. . . . They
urge us to be the answer to a hollow world." He laments,
"Today there is an abysmal ignorance of the most simple
and practical aspects of nearly all the classic Spiritual
Disciplines."[18]

This concept of discipline is uncommon in today's per-
missive society. Self-indulgence is preferred to self-mastery, feasting to fasting, superfluity to simplicity, confusion
to contemplation, self-seeking to self-giving.

The Book of Proverbs calls us to discipline. The word
occurs almost as many times in Proverbs as in the rest of
the Bible combined. The royal teacher declares, "Whoever loves discipline loves knowledge" (12:1) and, "He who

ignores discipline despises himself" (15:32). He also urges, "Get wisdom, discipline and understanding" (23:23). He is writing of the discipline that, by training and knowledge, will develop mastery and character.

Richard Foster defines a disciplined person as one who does what needs to be done when it needs to be done. This simple and yet incisive definition has the most practical applications for the Christian. The disciplined person rises a half hour earlier to allow time for the priority of morning devotions. The disciplined person resists watching television programs that would allow unholy scenes and thoughts to enter his mind. The disciplined person avoids the enticing foods that would impair health. The disciplined person makes the time and expends the effort for a needed exercise regimen. The disciplined person foregoes a luxury to avoid debt and is committed to a simple lifestyle. The disciplined person sacrifices the pleasure of the moment for the greater benefit of the future. The disciplined person has priorities in order and regulates life around them.

Wisdom to live by has a prerequisite of discipline. It is not a luxury for supersaints, but is the requirement for every believer. Jesus calls us to be disciples, to be a disciplined people. Discipline, states our text, leads to life. Then it must be true that the lack of discipline leads to death. Surely, there is no question which way we will choose, for we are on a quest for wisdom! We will dare to discipline.

> *Lord, in the words of Richard Foster I would pray, "Let me be among those who believe that the inner transformation of our lives is a goal worthy of my best effort."* [19]

TWENTY-FIVE

"DON'T TALK TOO MUCH"

Don't talk so much. You keep putting your foot in your mouth. Be sensible and turn off the flow! (10:19, TLB).

We are indebted to *The Living Bible* for this graphic and contemporary paraphrase of a proverb.

A Salvation Army publication of over 100 years ago offered this sage advice: " 'Brevity is the soul of wit,' so cut it short. If you have anything to say, say it, and then quit. . . . Long sermons are seldom heard through, so cut it short. They are never remembered, so cut it short. Don't tell all you know at any one time, but cut it short. Don't make long prayers in public, but cut it short. Do some of your praying in private so that in public you can cut it short." The wise writer of Proverbs who gave us the maxim, "Don't talk too much," would feel right at home with this advice.

It is not length but depth in speech that is important. It is not how long we may talk that counts, but what we have to say. An old preacher's prayer aptly expresses the virtue of brevity: "Lord, fill my mouth with worthwhile stuff, and stop me when I've said enough."

The most talkative person is often the one who has the least to say. The prudent person does not air his knowledge, but the shallow person loses no opportunity to proclaim his folly.

A stranger happened into a general store back in the hill country of Vermont. Coming from the hustle-bustle of the big city, he was quickly taken aback by the taciturnity that prevailed among the group sitting around. After what seemed to him an interminable silence, he felt constrained to ask, "Do you have an understanding here not to talk?" One of the natives replied, "No, we just don't say anything unless it improves on silence!"

Any further comment at this point would seem to only violate that good maxim!

Living Word, teach me an economy and discretion of speech that will make me fit and rewarding company in the social concourse of life.

TWENTY-SIX

GODLY CITIZENSHIP

*The good influence of godly citizens causes a city
to prosper, but the moral decay of the wicked drives
it downhill (11:11, TLB).*

"Godly citizenship" implies moral responsibility in the areas of government and commerce affecting our cities and nation. The Christian does not live in a private world, isolated from its realities, issues, and duties. He must exert his influence for good. This requires action, speaking up, initiative for the good of the community.

It is instructive to note that Jesus did not stay in the beautiful Galilean countryside. He took His message and ministry to Jerusalem. He lived in the city. He loved the city. He wept over the city (Luke 13:34). Similarly Paul took the Gospel to the great metropolises of his day: Damascus, Jerusalem, Caesarea, Rome. Moreover, the last book of the Bible reveals that the abode of the saints after our Lord's return will be the city of God, the "New Jerusalem." God calls us to be responsible citizens among our fellow beings who need the preserving influence of those called to be "the salt of the earth."

Responsible citizenship requires the intelligent exercise of our right to vote. "Godly citizens" will not be among the 50 percent of our country who do not go to the polls on election day. We will test and discern as much as possible the character and competence of political candidates. We will seek to affect the legislative process on the vital moral issues of our day. Let Christian voices be heard loud and clear on the issues that impact the moral life of our country and its citizens.

For example, one of the great scourges in our country is the ghastly evil of driving under the influence (DUI) of alcohol. This monster loose on the highways of our country kills 1 person every 23 minutes, 62 every day, over 25,000 a year. In the past decade it has slaughtered over a quarter million persons. This fiend further injures over 550,000 each year.[20] Drunk driving and other monstrous evils call for the concern and involvement of believers.

At the time of this writing the abortion issue hangs in the balance with the United States Supreme Court reviewing a case that could overthrow or alter the 1973 Roe v. Wade decision that has resulted in the silent holocaust of over 25 million legal abortions in the United States. At the same time a letter from my son, a Christian attorney, shares a copy of his telegram addressed to Justice Sandra Day O'Connor, who is believed to have the swing vote: "Like Queen Esther, who knows but that you have come to royal position for such a time as this? Save God's children."

The royal writer of Proverbs calls for godly citizens to be the salt that will stem the tide of pollution and be a preservative amid the decay that threatens to destroy us. Christian citizens, let us march forward to a better and brave new world!

Dag Hammarsjkold recorded in his diary, "The road to holiness necessarily passes through the world of action."[21] The Christian pilgrim travels always through a combat zone, with no demilitarized zone along the way. There are no pacifists in God's army. Let's each do something to make a difference and a better world.

God our strength, help us to employ all our energies and resources to "fight the good fight of faith."

TWENTY-SEVEN

THE PARADOX OF GIVING

One man gives freely, yet gains even more;
another withholds unduly, but comes to poverty
(11:24).

The Living Bible phrases this eloquent truth in colloquial
terms: "It is possible to give away and become richer! It
is also possible to hold on too tightly and lose everything.
Yes, the liberal man shall be rich! By watering others, he
waters himself."

Our western world too often becomes obsessed with
perquisites, possessions, and power. Proverbs offers anti-
dotes to the virus of materialism.

In my mother-in-law's Bible, there was found shortly
after her death, these words:

> What I spent, I had;
> What I gave, I have;
> What I kept, I lost.

Her liberality resulted in a spiritual legacy of inestimable worth. This proverb stresses that in life we have only
what we give away. Indeed, the one who gives gains; the
one who holds loses. As St. Francis penned in his prayer:
"It is in giving that we receive."

Edwin Markham, in his poem "There Is a Destiny," amplifies this truth in his lines:

There is a destiny that makes us brothers,
　　None lives to himself alone;
What we send into the lives of others
　　Comes back into our own.

God is the supreme Giver. God made the sun—it gives light and warmth. God made the moon—it gives beauty and radiance. God made the stars—they give majesty and order. God made the air—it gives sustenance and invigoration. God made the clouds—they give refreshing rain. God made the earth—it gives its bounty of food. God made the sea—it gives fish and pleasure. God made the trees—they give beauty, fuel, and usefulness. God made the flowers—they give fragrance. God made the birds— they give a song. God made the animals—they give variety. God made the plants—they give nourishment. God gave His Son—He gives salvation and life eternal. And God made you. What will you give?

I have not much to give Thee, Lord,
For that great love which made Thee mine.
I have not much to give Thee, Lord,
But all I have is Thine![22]
　　　　　　　　　　　　　—Richard Slater

TWENTY-EIGHT
THE WISEST ACT

He who wins souls is wise (11:30).

One more jewel gleams from this chapter for us to behold its beauty. Perhaps the greatest single achievement is to win a soul to Christ. We help that person come into the experience of life's deepest joy and fulfillment, knowledge of Christ as Savior and Lord, and the gift of life everlasting. No wonder God promised through His prophet Daniel: "Those who lead many to righteousness will shine like the stars for ever and ever" (Dan. 12:3).

E. Stanley Jones is considered by some one of the wisest men of past generations. Through his insightful and inspiring writings of twenty-eight books, he was a mentor to many of us. A world-renowned evangelist, Christian statesman, and author, several times nominated for the Nobel Peace Prize, he served as a missionary in his beloved India for over fifty years. When in his eighty-ninth year he had suffered a stroke that severely impaired his speech and sight and immobilized him, he confidently affirmed, just one month before going to be with his Lord:

> Now that I am in this crisis I face the question of living on crippled or calling it a day and accepting a

passage to the other world. . . . I don't know what the future holds, but I know who holds it. . . . I have often said half jokingly that when I get to heaven, I will ask for twenty-four hours to see my friends, and then I shall go up to Him and say, "Haven't you a world somewhere which has fallen people who need an evangelist like me? Please send me there." For I know no heaven beyond preaching the Gospel to people. That is heaven to me. It has been, is, and ever shall be heaven to me.[23]

"He who wins souls is wise." There is no greater achievement for time and eternity. Let's be counted among the wise.

"Lord, lay some soul upon my heart,
   And love that soul through me;
And may I humbly do my part
   To win that soul for Thee."
                         —Leon Tucker

TWENTY-NINE
BE KIND TO ANIMALS

A righteous man cares for the needs of his animal (12:10).

Amidst all these miscellaneous proverbs, we find one that will evoke an "amen" from every animal lover.

Stuart Hamblen testified that after he got saved even the chickens on the farm knew he was a different man.

Surely the One who identified Himself as the Good Shepherd, who at great sacrifice would seek out the lost sheep, would expect His followers to show love and responsible care for animals.

Animals are a remarkable creation of God. What pleasure and companionship pets have added to heart and home. What valued service their kind has given: a shepherd's dog, a seeing-eye dog, sled dogs, guardians of children and of the home. And who can estimate the contribution of dairy cattle, the horse, camel, elephant, sheep, goat, burro. And be ready for a eulogy if you ask a cat lover about the merits of his pet.

The astonishing imagination of God is revealed in His creation of the animal kingdom, its incredible variety from aardvarks to zebras. What marvelous creatures are the deer, fox, lion, hippopotamus, bear, kangaroo, tiger, as well as marine animals, reptiles, fish, birds. Books of zoology add volumes of testimony on the design and marvel of our world by our omniscient Creator.

Job, in his rebuttal to Zophar, citing nature as a witness of God to man, appealed: "But ask the animals, and they will teach you, or the birds of the air, and they will tell you . . . or let the fish of the sea inform you" (12:7-8). Quoting from my book *Portraits of Perseverance:*

> Ask a chipmunk with a body barely six inches long who made it able to carry and hide more than a bushel of acorns in just three days so he will be prepared for the long winter. Ask the snowshoe hare who turns its fur white only in the winter and the fawn who gave it spots to camouflage them from predators. Ask the sleek cheetah, the fastest land animal, who made it able to reach speeds of seventy miles an hour. Let the animals teach us of the marvelous endowments and providence of their Creator. . . .
>
> Ask millions of birds who endowed them with the marvel of migration as their feathered power takes them incredible distances, with the champion migrant, the small arctic tern, making an annual round trip of over 20,000 miles. Ask the ruby-throated hummingbird, weighing only an eighth of an ounce, who made it able to fly 500 miles across the Gulf of Mexico, its wings beating 50 times a second. Ask the birds and they will tell you who teaches them their solar and stellar navigation, who planted their inbuilt compasses enabling them to span continents and oceans. And ask the brown bat who enables it to emit sounds at 90,000 vibrations per second and, listening to the echo, to hunt and find its food on the wing. . . .

"Or let the fish of the sea inform you," added Job. The infinite variety, the incredible fecundity, and the exotic creations of marine life testify to a God of unlimited imagination and creativity.

Annie Dillard, in her delightful book *Pilgrim at Tin-*

ker Creek, writes, "The extravagant gesture is the very stuff of creation. . . . The whole show has been on fire from the word go. . . . Not only did the Creator create everything, but He is apt to create anything. He'll stop at nothing. . . . The Creator loves pizzazz." [24, 25]

Cecil Frances Alexander has expressed this truth in delightful verse:

All things bright and beautiful,
All creatures great and small,
All things wise and wonderful,
The Lord God made them all.

Help me, Lord, to have a responsible and caring oversight of animals, a very special gift You have given us.

THIRTY
THE POWER OF THE TONGUE

Reckless words pierce like a sword,
but the tongue of the wise brings healing (12:18).

"Speak that I may see thee," said Socrates. A strange statement. We would expect that he would have said, "Speak that I may hear thee." But the wise philosopher knew that people best reveal themselves by their speaking. Our words tell our world who we are. Every time we speak the world sees us.

Another wise philosopher, Emerson, reminds us that our words must correspond with our actions: "What you are stands over you the while and thunders so that I cannot hear what you say to the contrary."[26] How often have we seen actions belie words, where what a person has said just did not ring true with the life, where the image being projected did not square with the reality. John Bunyan described a character named Talkative as "a saint abroad and a devil at home." Words can either reveal or belie the all-important quality of authenticity. Indeed, our words reveal us to the world, for good or bad.

The New Testament Book of James describes the power of the tongue with graphic analogies. He illustrates his point repeatedly, pointing out that with a bit in a horse's mouth one can control this powerful animal, with a small rudder one can direct the course of a large ship, or with a

83

small spark one can ignite a huge forest and destroy it by fire. So the tongue, though small, is powerful and can control the person. James concludes, "No man can tame the tongue" and emphasizes his premise by stating, "If anyone is never at fault in what he says, he is a perfect man, able to keep his whole body in check" (James 3:2-8).

The royal writer of Proverbs in our text reveals the tongue's great power to hurt or heal:

Reckless words pierce like a sword,
but the tongue of the wise brings healing.

The tongue has great power to hurt. Unkind, careless words can wound. A devoted mother shared her deep hurt when one year her daughter-in-law announced, "This year we are are not going to observe Mother's Day." An aphorism reminds us: "Three things come not back— the spent arrow, the spoken word, and the lost opportunity." Once a word is spoken it can never be recalled. A careless word, an unkind comment, a rumor, a malicious story, all are impossible to obliterate.

But the tongue also has great power to heal. It can encourage, affirm, enrich, reconcile, forgive, unite, smooth, bless. Let us head the sage counsel of the proverb and have the tongue of the wise that brings healing.

One little unshed raindrop
May think itself too small;
Yet somewhere a thirsty flower
Awaits its fall.

One little word, unspoken,
May seem too small to say;
But somewhere, for that one word,
A heart may pray.
—Helen T. Allison

84

Jesus declared that our lives will be reckoned by our words, "For by your words you will be acquitted, and by your words you will be condemned" (Matt. 12:37). Let us weigh our words thoughtfully, prayerfully, and lovingly.

With the psalmist I pray, "Set a guard over my mouth, O Lord; keep watch over the door of my lips" (Ps. 141:3).

THIRTY-ONE
HEART TROUBLE

An anxious heart weighs a man down (12:25).

When the Book of Proverbs speaks about the heart it is never of the organ in our chest. Rather the writer employs a synecdoche—a figure of speech in which a part signifies the whole. The term *heart,* found eighty times in Proverbs, refers to our whole inner being—emotions, mind, and will. The Book of Proverbs identifies a number of heart disorders.

A "deceitful heart" is diagnosed in those who plot evil (12:20). A "sorrowful heart" can be present even when symptoms are absent, for "even in laughter the heart may ache" (14:13). These verses diagnose the tragic heart trouble of one who has been faithless, "The backslider in heart will be filled with his own ways" (14:14, NKJV). The "proud heart" is said to be detested by God (16:5). An "angry heart" against the Lord is also a sure symptom of folly (19:3). And the most fatal diagnosis of all is the "hardened heart" (28:14).

The spiritual cardiograph of our text diagnoses "an anxious heart" that "weighs a man down." Anxiety is, indeed, a heavy weight to carry. It borrows troubles and burdens of tomorrow, most of which never arrive. It suffers many side effects such as sleeplessness, headaches, strain, stress, and ulcers.

Anxiety and worry are the opposites of faith. The late Peter Marshall, chaplain of the U.S. Senate, once prayed at an opening of the Senate: "Help us to do our very best this day and be content with today's troubles, so that we shall not borrow the troubles of tomorrow. Save us from the sin of worrying, lest stomach ulcers be the badge of our lack of faith."[27]

There is a cure for anxiety. We have already encountered it in the Book of Proverbs. The divine prescription is to "trust in the Lord with all your heart and lean not on your own understanding" (3:5). Trust in God is the sure antidote for worry and anxiety.

When we trust our lives in His care and keeping, the Holy Spirit comes with the precious gift of peace within. The Apostle Paul expressed it memorably. "Do not be anxious about anything," he wrote, "but in everything, by prayer and petition, with thanksgiving, present your requests to God. And the peace of God, which transcends all understanding, will guard your hearts and your minds in Christ Jesus" (Phil. 4:6-7). The peace of God transcends not only our understanding, but misunderstandings as well.

We follow the One who promised, "My peace I give you. I do not give to you as the world gives. Do not let your hearts be troubled and do not be afraid" (John 14:27). Peace is one of the Lord's choicest gifts.

Do you suffer from heart trouble? Are you weighed down with some burden of worry and anxiety? If so, follow the prescription of the Great Physician — trust in God, and be spiritually hale, hearty and healthy.

Jesus came with peace to me,
His strong arm was stretched to me,
Then my burden took from me —
My Savior.[28]

—Agnes Heathcote

THIRTY-TWO

WASTED TROPHIES

The lazy man does not roast his game
but the diligent man prizes his possession (12:27).

This proverb pictures the hunter on an autumn morning out to greet the dawn. The air invigorates, the dogs sniff the scent. The excitement of the chase makes his adrenalin flow. His hand has not lost its cunning. The arrow finds its mark. He returns home with the prized bird he has brought down. So far all is well.

Then comes the waste, the sin. The morning's glow has evaporated. The bird lies until it is wasted. It is the sin of lost gains, of not giving the further effort required to conserve that over which toil was expended.

The hunter of Proverbs is not distant and far away. How many trophies have we known that were allowed to go to waste? The rich trophies sacrificially secured by parents, the treasures of a nation dearly bought, the riches of God's grace — all too often neglected, allowed to be lost when they could bring so much good. May we be careful not to waste the trophies and gains of life by neglect or lethargy.

I attended a funeral that was a celebration of a godly woman who helped raise an extraordinary family for God — the Rader family in The Salvation Army. All five children rose up that day in beautiful testimony to call their mother blessed. She had prayed and blessed the five children through sixty-two collective years of service on the missionary field. At the time of her funeral, her grandchildren were carrying on the family's tradition of overseas ministry. The service powerfully blessed the overflow attendance. Following the "Promotion to Glory" service, as we term it in the Army, I spoke with one of the lovely granddaughters and said to her, "What a beautiful heritage you have." Without hesitation she replied in a tone of dedication, "And what a responsibility to measure up to it."

When we acknowledge that we are debtors to gains of life that we inherit, and dedicate ourselves to faithful stewardship, we will acquit ourselves with honor to God and the world about us. The trophies of life will then shine all the brighter and bring their enrichment to us.

I am a heavy debtor, Lord, to so many who have bequeathed to me a noble heritage of faith. By Your Spirit make me more worthy and faithful.

THIRTY-THREE

HOPE DEFERRED — AND FULFILLED

Hope deferred makes the heart sick,
but a longing fulfilled is a tree of life (13:12).

"Hope deferred" is a common experience to all of us. It has been suggested that hopes too easily realized may not be worthy of the man whose "reach should exceed his grasp." A "hope deferred" should also be evaluated to assure that it is not merely selfish ambition or wishful thinking. The psalmist prayed: "Let me not be ashamed of my hope" (Ps. 119:116, NKJV).

Alexander Pope wrote, "Hope springs eternal in the human breast."[29] Emil Brunner begins his book *Eternal Hope* with the comparison, "What oxygen is for the lungs, such is hope for the meaning of human life." We can cope with the anguish of today if we know that things are going to come out right in the end. Man cannot live without hope.

A great hope and longing for world peace persists today. But peace is a hope deferred. The ominous clouds of nuclear holocaust hang over every new generation, causing many to be sick at heart. Hope exists for breakthroughs in medical science that will bring cures for dreaded diseases.

One of the great gifts of the Gospel is its hope to the believer. Christ and the New Testament gave a new dimension to hope. The writer of Hebrews wedded faith with hope: "Now faith is being sure of what we hope for" (Heb. 11:1). Hope requires faith and patience. A.J. Cronin wrote in one of his books that the true hell is not when hope is deferred but when people have ceased to hope.

History records a telling illustration on hope. The explorer Bartholomeu Dias in 1487 sailed farther than any had before him, going along the west coast of Africa. Coming upon a great promontory where he experienced severe winds and giant waves, he called it "The Cape of Storms." But his monarch, King John II of Portugal, saw in the discovery a new door opening a route to India. Consequently, he named it, "The Cape of Good Hope." History left to Vasco da Gama to sail around the cape in 1497 and arrive at Calicut, India.

Many people today see only the storms and the great waves of danger they bring. But others are filled with hope. Above all, Christians are those who "wait for the blessed hope—the glorious appearing of our great God and Savior, Jesus Christ" (Titus 2:13). That is the grandest hope of all, which has sustained Christians through the centuries. It will be as described in the second part of this proverb: "a longing fulfilled."

Thank You, God, that "I'm possessed of a hope that is steadfast and sure, since Jesus came into my heart."[30]

THIRTY-FOUR
"SPARE THE ROD"

He who spares the rod hates his son,
but he who loves him is careful to discipline him
(13:24).

Corporal punishment or spanking children has ignited controversy in recent years. Dr. James Dobson, writing of this subject, provides helpful insights and guidelines: "Corporal punishment in the hands of a loving parent is a teaching tool by which harmful behavior is inhibited." He points out that there is a place for minor pain in teaching children to behave responsibly.

Dr. Dobson offers ground rules for corporal punishment. "Mild spankings can begin between fifteen and eighteen months. They should be relatively infrequent and must be reserved for clear defiance, not childish irresponsibility. Spankings should be administered with a neutral object, but rarely with the hand which should be seen by the child as an object of love rather than an instrument of punishment."

There needs to be a clear distinction between discipline and abuse. Disciplining a child does not give license for venting anger or for extreme and unfair correction. True discipline confirms a parent's love for the child. They care enough to set healthy limits and to enforce the rules of good conduct and character. As our text affirms: *He who loves him [the child] is careful to discipline him.*

92

The writer of Hebrews in the New Testament draws an instructive analogy between a father's discipline of his children and God's discipline of us, summarizing, "God is treating you as sons. . . . God disciplines us for our good" (Heb. 12:5-11). The Apostle Paul, writing of family relationships, warns against severity on the part of fathers (Eph. 6:4).

The disciplining of children is a vital part of child rearing and training. But it must always be in the context of love, self-control, and discretion. Parents must love their children enough to say "no" and to correct them when needed. Firmness without love is harshness; love without firmness is softness. Love must be tender and tough.

Heavenly Father, help us love our children enough to say no, and discipline them always in love, self-control, and with discretion.

THIRTY-FIVE

LIVING TO EAT

The good man eats to live,
while the evil man lives to eat (13:25, TLB).

Discipline and discretion in eating habits should be a part of our Christian dedication and practice. God made eating to be a pleasurable experience. Like other pleasures, however, it requires certain disciplines and boundaries.

Obesity from overeating is a problem of epidemic proportions in the U.S. The National Institute of Health reports that about one out of five American adults is overweight. "Obesity is a killer," states the chairman, Dr. Jules Hirsch. Studies show that obese people have three times the normal incidence of high blood pressure and diabetes, an increased risk of heart disease, a shorter life span, and an unusually high risk of developing respiratory disorders, arthritis, and certain types of cancer. Physically speaking, we are largely what we eat (no pun intended!).

Gluttony has been labeled as an emotional escape, a sign that something is eating us. The person who "lives to eat" needs to find a higher purpose and priority for living.

We have been too slow to admit that our bodies and appetites are an intregral part of our consecration. We regard eating as a private domain, excluding God Himself. But God's Word says a great deal about the care of the body and gluttony. This proverb is just one of God's reminders. Another more forceful one suggests: "Put a knife to your throat if you are given to gluttony" (23:2).

Henry David Thoreau's journal offers the challenge: "Every man is a builder of a temple called his body. . . . We are all sculptors and painters, and our material is our flesh and blood and bone." The Apostle Paul commands, "Offer your bodies as living sacrifices, holy and pleasing to God – which is your spiritual worship" (Rom. 12:1). Making due allowance for physical, glandular, or other limitations, bodies that show the consequence of overindulgence or underexercise contradict the profession of a godly life.

Our society has a food fixation. Holidays are associated with eating orgies. We entertain with food; eating is an integral part of our social life. Enjoying food is proper; God designed us that way. But let us also keep in mind the Apostle Paul's admonition: "So whether you eat or drink or whatever you do, do it all for the glory of God" (1 Cor. 10:31).

Jesus Christ calls His followers to the highest and holiest, to be the best that we can be. He calls us from mediocrity to excellence, from softness to sanctification, from comfort to the Cross, from the supper room to the Upper Room. Let's get on with our pursuit of excellence!

Lord of all of life, grant me grace and discipline to always "offer my body as a living sacrifice, holy and pleasing to God – which is my spiritual worship."

THIRTY-SIX
THE END OF THE TRAIL

There is a way that seems right to a man,
but in the end it leads to death (14:12).

This is such an important truth that God repeats it in
16:25. It warns of self-deception in the way of sin. It is
rationalized, justified, excused. The person going down
the road of destruction is often blind to its peril. It "seems
right" to him. "But" – and that is always a word to reckon
with in these proverbs – "in the end it leads to death."

John Newton ran headlong down that road that leads
to death. He operated slave ships from Africa and lived a
profligate life. But in the depths of his sin and despair, he
turned to Christ and was transformed by His power. From
that experience he gave to Christendom one of its greatest songs:

> Amazing grace! how sweet the sound,
>   That saved a wretch like me!
> I once was lost, but now am found,
>   Was blind but now I see.
>
> 'Twas grace that taught my heart to fear,
>   And grace my fears relieved;
> How precious did that grace appear
>   The hour I first believed!

His self-written epitaph reads:

> John Newton, Clerk,
> Once an infidel and libertine,
> A servant of slaves in Africa,
> Was, by the rich mercy of our Lord and Savior,
> Jesus Christ
> Preserved, restored, pardoned
> And appointed to preach the faith he
> Had long labored to destroy.

Paul, who was to become the great professor of Christian theology, was going down the road to Damascus, a way that seemed right to him. But it was leading to death. On that road he met Christ, was turned in the opposite direction, and life was never the same.

But there are many who head down the road to destruction and do not seek Christ and a change of direction. Some think they will get saved at the eleventh hour, but they die at 10:30. The only way to life and liberty is to follow the One who announced, "I am the way.... No one comes to the Father except through Me" (John 14:6).

Christ the Way, all other ways are dead ends. My tomorrows, all known to You, are in Your hands to lead and guide.

THIRTY-SEVEN

HALLMARK OF A GREAT NATION

Righteousness exalts a nation,
but sin is a disgrace to any people (14:34).

What makes a nation great? Not military might, scientific advance, great prosperity, arts and culture—but rather it is righteousness which makes a nation great.

In *Breaking with Moscow,* Arkady Shevchenko, who had been a high-ranking Soviet diplomat, explains his defection from the Communist regime. He describes a system so interlaced with intrigue that "if Machiavelli were alive and living in the Soviet elite today, he would be a student, not a professor." Recounting his disillusionment, he tells how vice was called virtue and the words reversed again and "how their hypocrisy and corruption had penetrated their lives. . . . The falsity of these men was everywhere." Thus we have a testimony in our day to the second part of our proverb: "Sin is a disgrace to any people."

When we pray for our beloved country, may we pray above all that she will be a righteous nation, that she will honor the laws of God and reflect His love for others.

When in December 1989 Mikhail Gorbachev had his momentous meeting with Pope Paul II at the Vatican, he made the stunning announcement that the Soviet government would shortly pass a law guaranteeing religious freedom for all believers. Gorbachev in his speech in Rome spoke about the role of religion in terms that few people would ever have expected from a Kremlin leader. He stated: "We need spiritual values . . . this is the only way toward a new culture and new politics that can meet the challenge of our time. Now we not only proceed from the assumption that no one should interfere in matters of the individual's conscience; we also say that the moral values that religion generated and embodied for centuries can help in the work of renewal in our country."

This was a historic admission from the head of the foremost Communist country that had dictated a politics of atheism. How much more should we, in a country that was cradled in dependence on God, recognize the supreme importance of righteousness for our nation.

May our prayer ever be the one we offer in the words of the song, "God of Our Fathers," penned by Daniel C. Roberts:

Thy love divine hath led us in the past,
In this free land by Thee our lot is cast;
Be Thou our Ruler, Guardian, Guide and Stay,
Thy Word our law, Thy paths our chosen way.

Refresh Thy people on their toilsome way,
Lead us from night to never-ending day;
Fill all our lives with love and grace divine,
And glory, laud and praise be ever Thine.

Let us, Lord, indeed pray and work for those moral qualities that transcend the material and political and will make our nation truly great.

THIRTY-EIGHT

GENTLE WORDS

A gentle answer turns away wrath,
but a harsh word stirs up anger (15:1).

This is one of the most valued proverbs for practical application to life. How many situations require us to respond or react to unkindness, unfairness, disagreement, confrontation. In such encounters, a grievous word fuels the fire; a gracious word cools passions and builds a bridge to understanding.

Appeasement at any price is not recommended, but a studied, conciliatory approach that will assuage rather than exacerbate difficult relations. Once polemics or a war of words takes place, then reason and rapport are thrown to the wind.

Proverbs 15:1 is an essential guide for life. It is critically needed in the sensitive relationship between husband and wife, parent and child, employer and worker.

Some consider it a sign of weakness to allow hostile words or insult to go unchallenged. But gentle speech takes more power and character than unrestrained reaction. The greatest strength is often the power of restraint.

Our words wield incredible power. Countless lives have been discouraged and defeated due to an insensitive word. And many lives have gone on to triumph due to the word of encouragement.

A careless word may kindle strife;
A cruel word may wreck a life;
A bitter word may hate instill;
A brutal word may smite and kill;
A gracious word may smooth the way;
A joyous word may light the day;
A timely word may lessen stress;
A loving word may heal and bless.
—Author unknown

"Cold words freeze people," wrote Blaise Pascal, "and hot words scorch them, bitter words make them bitter, wrathful words make them wrathful. Kind words also produce their own image on men's souls, and a beautiful image it is. They soothe, quiet, and comfort the hearer." May we seek and know the grace of God in our speaking.

Sovereign God, who emptied Yourself and became obedient unto the very death of the cross, save me from false pride and grant to me, who am nothing apart from Your grace, the gift of humility.

THIRTY-NINE

THE GREAT DESTROYER

Pride goes before destruction,
a haughty spirit before a fall (16:18).

Pride caused the fall of Lucifer from heaven and has destroyed myriads of men and women.

Chuck Colson, in his classic spiritual autobiography, *Born Again,* tells of his deep struggle for peace during the crisis of Watergate. The turning point came when he visited his friend, Tom Phillips. After sharing his faith, Phillips said, "Chuck, I don't think you will understand what I'm saying about God until you are willing to face yourself honestly and squarely. This is the first step." He then gave to Chuck Colson C.S. Lewis' *Mere Christianity,* first reading to him this excerpt:

> There is one vice of which no man in the world is free; which everyone in the world loathes when he sees it in someone else; and of which hardly any people, except Christians, ever imagine they are guilty themselves. . . . There is no fault . . . which we are more unconscious of in ourselves. . . . The vice I am talking of is Pride. . . . Pride leads to every other vice: it is the complete anti-God state of mind.

Colson writes, "Suddenly I felt naked and unclean, my

bravado defenses gone. I was exposed, unprotected, for Lewis' words were describing me."[31]

Pride is a denial of our creatureliness, a declaration of independence from God. How prone we are to think of ourselves as self-sufficient, to rely on our expertise, organization, schemes, technology. We need a theology of weakness as an antidote to pride. Our true strength and adequacy is found alone in Paul's paradoxical claim: "When I am weak, then I am strong" (2 Cor. 12:10).

The sage of Proverbs gave his diagnosis centuries earlier. Pride will lead us to destruction and a haughty spirit will cause us to fall. Only the Celestial Surgeon can excise this spiritual cancer and help us toward humility and love. Calvary provided the cure.

Divine Wisdom, lead me to unlearn my unwise ways of pride and self-reliance and to come to a knowledge that You are my sufficiency.

FORTY
THE GREATEST CONQUEST

He that is slow to anger is better than the mighty;
and he that ruleth his spirit than he that taketh
a city (16:32, NKJV).

The highest human achievement, in the day when the Book of Proverbs was written, was the conquest of a city. The pages of history abound with accounts telling how, either by slow siege or sudden assault, the walls of a city were stormed and its inhabitants conquered. Mounted on his war charger or swaying in his gilded chariot, the conqueror would make his triumphal entry to the cheers of his army. It was the utmost of human endeavors in that day, the most renowned of the exploits of men.

But even in that remote age, when the conqueror of a city was the greatest figure on the human horizon, the inspired writer of Proverbs saw that there was a greater conquest and a more ultimate victory—the conquest of self. The most imperial of cities is that of the human heart. He who is able to rule this city, says the penman of Proverbs, is the greatest of all conquerors.

Who usually causes us our most difficulty? Who gives us the most trouble? Dwight L. Moody said, "I have had more trouble with Dwight L. Moody than anyone else. If I can keep him straight I will be all right."

In Leningrad there is a magnificent equestrian statue of

Peter the Great with his hand uplifted, pointing his nation toward the sea. He was truly one of the great rulers of his country and helped mold modern Russia. But he was subject to maniacal outbursts of fury and rage, in one of which he killed his own son. Toward the end of his life Peter the Great said, "I have conquered an empire, but I was not able to conquer myself."

It is still true that the noblest conquest is self-conquest, the highest mastery is self-mastery. The control of temper and the passions of life demand our utmost effort and discipline.

The Apostle Paul had many enemies, suffering persecution and hardship. But who does he identify as giving him his most difficult struggle? Listen in on his moving spiritual autobiography: "It is I who am carnal, and have sold my soul to sin. In practice, what happens? My own behavior baffles me. For I find myself not doing what I really want to do but doing what I really loathe . . . an unwilling prisoner to the law of sin and death. It is an agonizing situation, and who on earth can set me free from the clutches of my own sinful nature?" (Rom. 7:14-24, PH). Paul's own behavior, which greatly baffled him, and the carnal nature he had found within gave him far more trouble and agony than the many other opponents he faced.

Edwin L. Sabin has put it dramatically in his poem "An Enemy I Had":

> An enemy I had, whose mien
> I stoutly strove in vain to know;
> For hard he dogged my steps, unseen,
> Wherever I might go.
>
> My plans he balked; my aims he foiled;
> He blocked my every onward way.
> When for some lofty goal I toiled,
> He grimly said me nay.

105

"Come forth!" I cried, "Lay bare thy guise!
Thy wretched features I would see."
Yet always to my straining eyes
He dwelt in mystery.

Until one night I held him fast,
The veil from off his form did draw;
I gazed upon his face at last —
And, lo! myself I saw.

Browning's words come to mind, "When the fight begins within himself, a man's worth something."[32] How true of our troubles is the oft-repeated statement, "I have no one to blame but myself."

How do we achieve victory over ourselves? How do we come to self-mastery? The secret is given in the New Testament: "The fruit of the Spirit is . . . self-control" (Gal. 5:22, 23). When we surrender to His leading, the power of the Holy Spirit breaks the clutches of our sinful nature within and gives us victory over ourselves.

Let's go forth and be even greater than an Alexander, a Caesar, and all those conquerors of cities!

Thank You, God, for the promise of Scripture that "I can do all things through Christ who strengthens me" (Phil. 4:13).

FORTY-ONE

THE CROWN JEWELS OF GRANDCHILDREN

Children's children are a crown to the aged,
and parents are the pride of their children (17:6).

James Herriot, every reader's favorite veterinarian, reflects a special insight with children as well as with animals: "I'm into a lower gear now. Life's passing by and I'm getting into the last lap. I missed my children's childhood, and I don't want to miss my grandchildren's childhood" (from *The Lord God Made Them All*).

God gives a special blessing after our own children are grown and flown, in the joy of relationship with children all over again. It makes the "last laps" of life joyful. Grandchildren are indeed the "crown to the aged." And with typical bias as a grandparent, I often refer to our eleven very special gifts as the "crown jewels" of our life.

Grandparents provide a living link between the wisdom of yesterday and the needs of youth today. Carole Streeter, in her book *Reflections for Women Alone,* quotes from Page Smith's *Daughters of the Promised Land* in pointing out that grandparents have a vital role of mediating between the child and his parents. The grandmother's "stories of the child's parents' childhood made the parents understandably human for the child, gave them a stronger reality as people whose lives had a depth and texture not readily revealed in day-to-day relations

107

within the family. It is always an enthralling experience for a child to discover the childhood of its parents."[33]

Salvationist poet Mary J. Miller penned a tribute to the grandmother of our eleven jewels as well as to all her kind in her poem "Grandmothers":

> Grandmothers love us in so many ways
> That bring delight to all our days;
> They kiss our hurts and make them well;
> They know that secrets are not to tell,
> They are patient with our wildest schemes;
> They cherish all our fondest dreams;
> They teach us that life will not always be fair,
> But that Grandmother's arms will always be there.
>
> The "Grand" in Grandmothers is no disguise,
> They make life grand with sweet surprise . . .
> God's grand dose of joy, to ease life's growing pain,
> Is a child in Grandmother's arms again.[34]

What untold blessings are forfeited by those whose life-styles are too career-oriented to have children. They miss out on the greatest riches of life—children and grandchildren.

Indeed, "Children's children are a crown to the aged." But that's only one side of the coin of this golden text. The other is that "parents are the pride of their children." If we are faithful we end up doubly blessed—the joy of our children's children and the pride of our children.

What a tragedy when children cannot be proud of their parents. May God help us be faithful to this, life's highest priority, life's most sacred trust. Then the rich blessings of this text will be our heritage.

Thank You, God, for the joy and trust of grandchildren and for parents whose love and faith give reason for pride and gratitude. Help us be worthy of these sacred honors.

FORTY-TWO
GO AHEAD, LAUGH

A cheerful heart does good like medicine,
but a broken spirit makes one sick (17:22, NKJV).

He was given a 1 in 500 chance of survival upon diagnosis of his disease. The prognosis: a degenerative spinal condition; time to finalize his will. That was in 1964. But instead, Norman Cousins turned to an unorthodox therapy. He took massive doses of laughter. He secured and watched Marx Brothers' movies and "Candid Camera" reruns and found that laughter gave him pain-free sleep. He continued laughing. As he describes in his well-known book, his symptoms disappeared. He was cured.[35]

Medical science is now finding that laughter is good medicine. It is especially effective in fighting infections, stress, headaches, arthritis, gout, chronic allergies. "Bring in the clowns" may become a reality in medical units of the future!

Mr. Cousins merely put into practice what the sage of Proverbs wrote almost 3,000 years earlier. He and others have discovered that "there ain't much fun in medicine, but there's a lot of medicine in fun."

Laughter is good for body and soul. God made us to laugh, as surely as He made us to breathe and to cry.

Stern, dour, gloomy personalities are a far cry from the life and teachings of the One who said, "I have come that they may have life, and that they may have it more abundantly" (John 10:10, NKJV). At times it is as sacred to laugh as to witness or worship.

Indeed, laughter can be a form of witness and worship. We can worship God with our joy and exhilaration, and we can witness by the ecstasy He has put in our lives.

Beware of any frowning fraternity of modern day Pharisees who take themselves, life, and religion too seriously. With Teresa of Avila we pray, "From sour-faced saints, good Lord, deliver us."

God calls us to be winsome witnesses, to reflect and pass on the unspeakable joy He has given us.

If you've been missing out on the therapy of laughter, put it on your daily agenda. There are good starters all around you. In fact, we don't have to go far at all. We can start right with ourselves! Go ahead, laugh!

> *God, whose humor is revealed in the design of a camel and the playfulness of a kitten, teach me the art of not taking myself too seriously, to laugh heartily and be a winsome witness.*

TALK IS NOT CHEAP

The tongue has the power of life and death (18:21).

Xanthus, the philosopher, told his servant that on the morrow he was going to have some friends to dine, and ordered him to obtain the finest things he could find in the market to serve. The philosopher and his guests sat down the next day at the table. The menu featured tongue—nothing but tongue—four or five identical courses. The philosopher lost his patience and upbraided his servant, "Didn't I tell you to get the best thing in the market?" The servant replied, "I did get the best thing in the market. Isn't the tongue the organ of sociality, the organ of eloquence, the organ of kindness, the organ of worship?"

Then Xanthus said: "Tomorrow I want you to get the worst thing in the market." And on the morrow the philosopher sat at the table, and there was nothing but tongue—four or five courses of tongue! He again lost his patience and said, "Didn't I tell you to get the worst thing in the market?" The servant replied, "I did; for isn't the tongue the organ of blasphemy, the organ of defamation, the organ of lying?"

The son of David, whose proverbs made him the literary prodigy of his time, expressed this truth, "The tongue has the power of life and death." The awesome power of life and death that resides in the tongue makes it a lethal weapon. The sage of Proverbs had a great deal to say about speech. The terms *tongue, lips, mouth,* and *words* are found nearly 150 times in Proverbs.

Talk is never cheap. Think of the reverberations of Lincoln's Gettysburg Address and Churchill's "blood, toil, tears, and sweat." Pindar, writing in the fifth century B.C., observed, "Longer than deeds liveth the word."[36] All co-operation between human beings depends upon communication. No undertaking involving others is ever begun without an exchange of words.

Our words in large measure convey the impact and influence of our lives. Words have been known to start wars, bring marriage conflicts, fracture human relationships, and create misunderstandings. Words also have helped, healed, cheered, and made the difference between defeat and victory in someone's life.

The Apostle Paul's words to the church at Ephesus give us the model for our speaking: "Do not let any unwholesome talk come out of your mouths, but only what is helpful for building others up according to their needs, that it may benefit those who listen" (Eph. 4:29).

> *Lord, speak to me that I may speak*
> *In living echoes of Thy tone.*
>   *—Frances Ridley Havergal*

FORTY-FOUR

THE BEST OF LIFE

*The glory of young men is their strength;
of old men, their experience (20:29, TLB).*

"The Father said to me when I passed seventy: 'I'm giving you the best ten years of your life—the next ten ahead.' Two of them have passed and they have literally been the best two years of my life. . . . Practically all my question marks have now been straightened out into dancing exclamation points."[37] Thus E. Stanley Jones testifies to the truth of this proverb in his book *Christian Maturity.*

Robert Browning expressed this truth in unforgettable lines:

> Grow old along with me,
> The best is yet to be;
> The last of life
> For which the first was made;
> Our times are in His hand
> Who saith, "A whole I planned,
> Youth shows but half; Trust God,
> See all, nor be afraid!"[38]

On your sixty-fifth birthday, earlier for some, a voice will whisper, "Fold your oars and drift. You've done enough with your life, relax. Don't go out in the rain."

113

Temptation rears to rock away the years like "Whistler's Mother." Utopia is sitting before a screen and idling the days away. "You can't teach old dogs new tricks" becomes a text with unction. Such a life of innocuous leisure is mocked by the valued experience the aged bring as stated by the royal recorder of wisdom to live by: "The glory of old men is their experience."

Caleb, when eighty-five years young, asked for a hard task as a favor (Josh. 14:12). He and Joshua, the oldest in the Israelite camp, had survived the forty-year death march in the wilderness. But every new sunrise was to him a call to action and achievement. "Give me another mountain," he says, "and I will go and conquer it for the Lord."

There is no retirement plan suggested in the Bible, no need to settle down for a humdrum round of creature comforts. The Christian, in his later years, does not yield to those two thieves—regret for the past and fear for tomorrow. With Victor Hugo one can say: "Winter is on my head, but eternal spring is in my heart. The nearer I approach the end, the plainer I hear around me the immortal symphonies of the worlds which invite me."

When we come to the golden years, let us as Caleb, look for new mountains to climb. With the psalmist, we can confidently affirm: "They will still bear fruit in old age, they will stay fresh and green, proclaiming, 'The Lord is upright' " (Ps. 92:14-15).

Thank You, God, for the peerless glory of autumn and for the uncommon beauty of life's golden years.

FORTY-FIVE

A NAGGING WIFE

Better to live in a desert
than with a quarrelsome and ill-tempered wife
(21:19).

One of the more intriguing characters who slips in and out of the Proverbs is the quarrelsome or nagging wife. She makes her entrance and exit no less than five times from the stage of this book. "A quarrelsome wife is like a constant dripping" (19:13), "Better to live on a corner of the roof than share a house with a quarrelsome wife" (21:9), "Better to live in a desert than with a quarrelsome and ill-tempered wife" (21:19), "Better to live on a corner of the roof than share a house with a quarrelsome wife" (25:24) and "A quarrelsome wife is like a constant dripping on a rainy day; restraining her is like restraining the wind or grasping oil with the hand" (27:15-16).

Solomon apparently had a domestic problem! Serves him right for having all those wives, 700 of them! (1 Kings 11:3) With that many women getting in each other's way, they may even have had something to be quarrelsome about! But apart from Solomon's harem, the couplets present an enduring truth.

Many today would wholeheartedly agree (those of a certain gender, of course) that it would be better to accept privation and severe discomfort—"to live on a corner of a roof" or "in a desert"—than to be vexed by a nagging wife. Give such a brawling woman a lot of space, writes David's son. Her nagging is tormenting like a water drip that will not go away. (Too bad women did not write proverbs in those days. Mrs. Solomon no doubt could have penned a few good ones of her own!)

This was apparently such a common subject, among men of course, that there was an Arab proverb: "Three things make a home intolerable—*tak* (leaking rain), *nak* (nagging wife), and *bak* (bugs)!" A modern story is told of a man married to a fastidious wife. He got out of bed one night for a midnight snack, and when he came back to bed, she had it made!

These proverbs make their point. Nagging and quarrel-someness are tormenting and disruptive to a home. If the husband seems to be in need of being made over, listen to the wise words of Ruth Graham: "It's my job to love Billy. It's God's job to make him good."

Lord, make me pleasant and easy to live with.

116

FORTY-SIX

A GOOD NAME

A good name is more desirable than great riches; to be esteemed is better than silver or gold (22:1).

A person's name and reputation are of far greater value than any earthly possessions. Reputation is a priceless treasure, to be diligently guarded by uncompromising character and integrity.

In *Othello,* Shakespeare puts this truth in perspective:

"Good name in man and woman, dear my Lord,
  Is the immediate jewel of their souls;
Who steals my purse steals trash; 'tis something, nothing;
'Twas mine, 'tis his, and has been slave to thousands;
But he that filches from me my good name
  Robs me of that which not enriches him,
  And makes me poor indeed.

We live in a day that is very image conscious. Public relations firms are paid large sums to polish, protect, and project the best images for their clients. Many Christians get caught up in the image syndrome. We want to make a good impression. We cultivate and nurture our image. We work hard on an image that shows us to be good, gracious and sometimes, great.

Some years ago I heard the late General Frederick Coutts of The Salvation Army preach to a large gathering in Westminster Hall, London. He made a statement that indelibly impressed itself on me. He said, "Take care of the reality and the image will take care of itself." What profound counsel! What a life-affirming truth! What a landmark to guide us on our pilgrim way!

Reputation is one of the greatest assets of the Christian. It is what gives credibility, bestows confidence, gains acceptance, and opens opportunity. But reputation is the external. It is the print of what we really are, the outgrowth of the roots of our reality.

Let us so live that we will have a good name—springing forth from the reality of our relationship with Christ.

Crystal Christ, help me to ever care for the reality and let the image take care of itself.

FORTY-SEVEN
TRAIN A CHILD

Train a child in the way he should go,
and when he is old he will not turn from it (22:6).

The saying of the Jesuit, "Give me your child till he is twelve, and I care not who has charge of him afterwards," has passed into a proverb. The tree follows the bent of its early years and so do our sons and daughters, as the proverb preaches.

There is a "way" we should all go. It is the way of life. It is the direction of our destiny. Many miss it. All other ways lead to death.

But we do not go the way of life as a natural course. We need encouragement, training, guidance. God has given parents that most sacred trust of all—the training of our children so they will go in His way for them. It is our highest honor and priority.

Training involves a discipline of the child. That is one of the most consistent themes of the Book of Proverbs.

M. Scott Peck, in his best-seller *The Road Less Traveled,* writes of meaningless discipline when "parents serve as undisciplined role models for their children. They are the 'Do as I say, not as I do' parents. . . . They may fight with each other in front of the children without restraint, dignity or rationality. They may be slovenly. They make promises they don't keep . . . and their attempts to order the lives of their children seem therefore to make little sense to these children."[39] The training and discipline of children need the reinforcement of our example. They will be most influenced by what they see in us.

We have heard busy parents say, "We don't get to spend much time with our children but make it up by having 'quality' time when we do get together." Dr. James Dobson says of this phrase bandied about by over-committed parents: "I maintain that this convenient generalization simply won't hold water."

He goes on to argue his case: "Let's suppose you are very hungry," he says, "having eaten nothing all day. You select the best restaurant in your city and ask the waiter for the finest steak on his menu. He replies that the filet mignon is the house favorite, and you order it charcoal-broiled, medium rare. The waiter returns twenty minutes later with the fare and sets it before you. There in the center of a large plate is a lone piece of meat, one inch square, flanked by a single bit of potato. You complain vigorously. He replies . . . 'I have brought you one square inch of the finest steak money can buy. It is cooked to perfection. . . . I'll admit that the serving is small, but after all, sir, everyone knows that it isn't the quantity that matters; it's the quality that counts in steak dinners.' . . . Nonsense. . . . It is insufficient to toss our 'hungry' children an occasional bite of steak, even if it is prime, corn-fed filet mignon."

May we who are parents dedicate ourselves to giving the quantity and the quality of time deserved for the training of our children. They may even depart for a time from that training, but God promises, if we are faithful, "when he is old he will not turn from it."

The words of Dorothy Nolte make a worthy appendage to our text:

If a child lives with criticism, he learns to condemn.
If a child lives with hostility, he learns to fight.

If a child lives with ridicule, he learns to be shy.
If a child lives with shame, he learns to feel guilty.
If a child lives with tolerance, he learns to be patient.
If a child lives with encouragement, he learns
confidence.
If a child lives with praise, he learns to appreciate.
If a child lives with fairness, he learns justice.
If a child lives with security, he learns to have faith.
If a child lives with approval, he learns to like
himself.
If a child lives with acceptance and friendship, he
learns to find love in the world.[40]

Is there any higher claim on our time and energy than the training of our children? Is there any activity which brings greater reward? Then let's get on with it!

Heavenly Father, keep us faithful in the sacred trust and priority of training our children in the way they should go.

FORTY-EIGHT
REMOVE NOT ANCIENT LANDMARKS

*Do not remove an ancient boundary stone
set up by your forefathers (22:28).*

Ancient landmarks or boundary stones were held to be
sacred in the ancient world. Our text harks back to the
Mosaic Code which warned, "Do not move your neighbor's boundary stone" (Deut. 19:14). It is repeated in
Proverbs, being also found in 23:10. Such stones were
erected to indicate the perimeters of fields and estates.
Moving them illegally to increase one's own holdings
constituted a serious crime. The tourist in Israel can still
see today mounds of stones as boundary markers.

The landmarks placed by those who had lived before
were deemed sacred. This text holds a special message
for our era of kaleidoscopic change where the new is
often held up as the ideal and the old is considered out-
moded, to be discarded. Alvin Toffler in *Future Shock*
writes of "the death of permanence" and mourns that
"we are all citizens of the Age of Transience." Toffler
describes the economics of impermanence as giving rise
to disposability—the spread of the throw-away culture
and the ephemeralization of man's links with the things
that surround him.[41]

Indeed, the ancient landmarks are not only being re-
moved, but obliterated.

It is true that traditions of the past hold not only profit but peril. They can freeze progress. Their epitaph reads, "We have never done it this way before." They can lock us into a flawed philosophy or a sterile system. But let's not "throw away the baby with the bathwater."

We are all heavy debtors to the past. We owe an incalculable debt to generations who have paid the high cost of discipleship for our privileged possession of the Bible, freedom of worship, and writings that have been sources of priceless inspiration. The centuries instruct the years and we need to tap the rich reservoir of the past, the legacy of thought and experience that has preceded us.

Longfellow wrote:

> Lives of great men all remind us
>   We too can make our lives sublime
> And departing leave behind us
>   Footprints in the sands of time;
> Footprints, that perhaps another,
>   Sailing o'er life's solemn main,
> A forlorn and shipwrecked brother,
>   Seeing, shall take heart again.[42]

For each of us there are voices from the past that we need to hear and heed. There are landmarks and traditions that must remain sacred. Sacred landmarks have been set down by parents, grandparents, loved ones, friends. The rich traditions of our church with its landmarks are greatly needed in this day of moral confusion and chaos. We need to know the moral boundaries of life around us for we live in enemy-occupied territory.

Let us take care not to remove the ancient landmarks for our life, lest we lose our way on life's pilgrimage.

Keep me true, Lord, to the faith of our fathers; grant that I will ever prize my heritage and be guided by the sacred landmarks of my life.

123

FORTY-NINE
OUR HEART'S SUITOR

My son, give me your heart (23:26).

"My son, give me your heart" is the plea and longing of a
father that echoes across the centuries to strike a respon-
sive chord with every parent. Fathers long for the affection, love, and loyalty of their children.

This appeal also comes from the Divine Suitor. To each
of us He calls, "Give Me your heart."

"Give Me your heart" is the gracious invitation of Christ
to each of us. He woos us by His infinite love. He entreats
us by His unspeakable sacrifice. He calls us by the tender
promptings of the Holy Spirit. Jesus summarized all the
commandments in one simple, yet sublime statement:
"Love the Lord your God with all your heart and with all
your soul and with all your mind" (Matt. 22:37). Loving
God wholeheartedly is the ultimate purpose and fulfillment of life.

Napoleon, from his prison on St. Helena, recorded this
impression of Christ: "I have inspired multitudes with
such devotion that they would have died for me. But to
do this it was necessary that I should be visibly present,
with the electric influences of my looks, of my words, of
my voice.

"Christ alone has succeeded in so raising the mind of

124

man toward the unseen that it becomes insensible to the barriers of time and space. Across a chasm of eighteen hundred years Jesus Christ makes a demand which is, above all others, difficult to satisfy. He asks for that which a philosopher may often seek in vain at the hands of his friends, or a father of his children, or a bride of her spouse. He asks for the human heart. He demands it unconditionally, and forthwith His demand is granted. In defiance of time and space, the soul of man with all its powers becomes an annexation to the empire of Christ.

"This phenomenon is unaccountable; it is altogether beyond the scope of man's creative powers. This it is which strikes me most. I have often thought of it. That it is which proves to me quite conclusively the divinity of Jesus Christ."

The greatest love story of the world is capsulized in John 3:16: "For God so loved the world that He gave His one and only Son, that whoever believes in him shall not perish but have eternal life." Such love surpasses our understanding, but it wins our hearts!

All my heart I give Thee,
  Day by day, come what may,
All my life I give Thee,
  Dying men to save. [43]

FIFTY

THE CURSE OF STRONG DRINK

In the end it bites like a snake
and poisons like a viper (23:32).

Six questions are asked in the twenty-third chapter of Proverbs. They deal with human calamities — woe, sorrow, strife, complaints, bruises, bloodshot eyes. "Who has woe? Who has sorrow? Who has strife? Who has complaints? Who has needless bruises? Who has bloodshot eyes?" (23:29).

Do you recognize the symptoms? They are the same today. The answer is given: "Those who linger over wine" (23:30).

Alcoholism is one of the great curses of man. "It drives men to hell," wrote John Wesley. "It is more destructive than war, pestilence, and famine," said Gladstone. Abraham Lincoln described it as "a cancer in human society."

Drunkenness has spawned more crime, caused more poverty, ruined more families, degraded more men and women, and put more men behind prison bars than any other single curse. It is a deadly foe to the home, the church, the state, and the individual. It wreaks degradation and destruction.

One of its worst sins is its over 26,000 victims each year killed in drunken-driving auto accidents in the U.S. Its curse is all too often inflicted on the innocent.

The sage of Proverbs describes its enticement "when it sparkles in the cup, when it goes down smoothly!" (23:31) But he also paints the horrid picture of its consequences:

> In the end it bites like a snake
> and poisons like a viper.
> Your eyes will see strange sights
> and your mind imagine confusing things.
> You will be like one sleeping on the high seas,
> lying on the top of the rigging.
> "They hit me," you will say, "but I'm not hurt!
> They beat me, but I don't feel it!
> When will I wake up so I can find another drink?"
> (23:32-35)

All the ingredients of drunkenness are there—its poison, stupor and confusion, nausea, unawareness of inflicted violence, uncontrolled craving for "another drink."

The seductive sparkle turns to poison, its promised enchantment becomes a venomous reptile whose bite brings on delirium and destruction.

For over 100 years The Salvation Army has taken a position, not of moderation, but of total abstinence. It has all too often seen the horrible effects of drink upon individuals and families. Anyone with this problem should seek and find God's help to solve it. The power of God has reclaimed the lives of many who have called upon Him to break the strong hold of drink upon them, which they could not have done on their own.

Almighty God, just now I pray by name for the one I know is struggling with the problem of alcohol. Help that person seek and find Your power to break free of its powerful hold and curse.

FIFTY-ONE

THE ENDURING WORD

These are more proverbs of Solomon,
copied by the men of Hezekiah king of Judah (25:1).

Most of Solomon's 3,000 proverbs and 1,005 songs (1 Kings 4:32) are lost to us. All the proverbs are attributed to Solomon except for those in 22:17–24:23 (which are attributed to "the wise men") and chapters 30 and 31, assigned to Agur and Lemuel, respectively. Thus, Solomon wrote 780 of the Proverbs, plus his dirge of Ecclesiastes, his love lyrics of the Song of Solomon, and Psalm 127.

Perhaps these statistics may offer instruction. God only will preserve what is for His glory.

The five chapters, 25–29, contain proverbs that King Hezekiah's staff collected some 250 years after Solomon wrote them, no doubt as part of the reforms and revival during the reign of Hezekiah. Even such a famous king and literary prodigy as Solomon needed others, centuries later in this instance, to assure the outcome of his work. We are all dependent upon the effort of others to help give meaning for our lives.

And, of course, all of us who take up the pen, or today work with the wizardry of the computer, are debtors to many others who have either been our tutors or enablers. The "acknowledgment" page of any book mentions only a fraction of those to whom the credit is due. All our writing must own the inspiration and anointing of the Ultimate Editor in Chief if it is to have true meaning.

Fulton Sheen, in his autobiography, tells of an Emmy Awards ceremony where each recipient thanked producers, directors, friends, colleagues, and assistants. He records, "When my name was called out for an award, I was momentarily lost for words and then it struck me. Since everyone was thanking others, I should say a word of thanks too. 'I wish to thank my four writers, Matthew, Mark, Luke, and John.' "[44]

Our Lord placed a high value on the inspired truths of Proverbs. His parable in Luke 14:7-11 is obviously based on this proverb: "Do not claim a place among great men; it is better for him to say to you, 'Come up here,' than for him to humiliate you before a nobleman" (25:6-7).

The person with pride and love of prominence will no doubt rate himself higher than others do. Such pride can lead to bumptious behavior, giving airs of a dignity and rank not in fact accorded him. If he stakes his claim to precedence in the ranks of notables, he risks the rebuff.

As Jesus also put it, it is better to occupy a place lower than your entitlement and then be called higher than to suffer loss of face for promoting yourself beyond the limits of your position.

A loving daughter, in a tribute to a godly mother, eulogized, "She never sought the high places, but she always traveled on the high road." Such is the calling of every Christian.

Help me, Lord, not to seek the high places for myself, but to always travel on the high road of holiness and love.

FIFTY-TWO
GOD'S SECRETS

It is the glory of God to conceal a matter:
to search out a matter is the glory of kings (25:2).

This proverb portrays the dramatic contrast between God and man. God's ways are inscrutable, clothed in mystery, inaccessible to research. "His understanding no one can fathom" (Isa. 40:28).

But the success of man requires examination, investigation of all the facts. His ways are discernible, explicable.

God never advertises Himself in His works. As someone has beautifully expressed it, "He paints the wayside flower and lights the evening star, and leaves them to be His silent witnesses. He places His song in the throats of singing birds, in the sound of waterfalls and streams, and in the crash of heavy seas against cliffs, and hides behind them all."

As the old theology books put it, "God is a mystery." He exists in unapproachable majesty and holiness. His works of creation are done in silence and without fanfare. A breathtaking sunrise bursts upon the earth in total stillness. The star-strewn spaces of the heavens shine resplendent without noise or sound. God's glory is concealed in the profound silences of swirling worlds and infinite cosmos.

130

The Psalms enshrine a beautiful contrasting truth. "The Lord confides in those who fear Him; He makes His covenant known to them" (25:14). Although it is the glory of God to conceal a matter, He reveals His secrets to those who revere and love Him. He takes them into His confidence.

How marvelous—God tells us His secrets. He becomes, as other translations put it, "intimate with those who fear Him." To the pure in heart are vouchsafed the secrets of the eternal God. Imagine, the God of the universe becoming personal and intimate with you and me. He tells us that He loves us and wants to live in our hearts forever. What marvelous condescension. What amazing grace!

Albert Orsborn, the late Poet General of The Salvation Army, has expressed this experience in devotional verse:

In the secret of Thy presence,
  Where the pure in heart may dwell,
Are the springs of sacred service
  And a power that none can tell.
There my love must bring its offering,
  There my heart must yield its praise,
And the Lord will come, revealing
  All the secrets of His ways.[45]

God of majesty and mystery, with the poet I pray, "In the secret of Thy presence, in the hiding of Thy power, let me love Thee, let me serve Thee, every consecrated hour."

FIFTY-THREE
A WORD APTLY SPOKEN

*A word aptly spoken is like apples of gold
in settings of silver (25:11).*

For those of us who have fallen captive to the charm and magic of words, this proverb has become a "golden rule" to strive for in speech and writing.

Conjure up in your imagination the beautiful picture of this striking simile — "apples of gold in settings of silver." It delights and titillates "the mind's eye." It pays a high compliment to "a word aptly spoken." Such a well-chosen and well-shaped word is celebrated as an exquisite object of art.

We all enjoy that rare and refreshing stroll down the picturesque path of well-chosen words. Shakespeare, writing with a whittled quill by the light of a tallow candle, produced lines that will be read till the end of time. He knew the discipline and delight of "a word aptly spoken." A commonplace writer would have said that a certain thing would "be superfluous, like trying to improve the perfect." In his *King John*, Shakespeare expressed the same thought with a picture-phrase that is immortal:

To gild refined gold, to paint the lily,
to throw perfume on the violet.

Such writing and speech are arts of the highest form. A cat with a ball of wool is a graceless thing compared to a craftsman with a fistful of words!

The Bible itself is the greatest example of our proverb. Its memorable phrases have been engraved on the hearts and minds of men through the centuries, memorized, quoted, lived. God adorned His message to man in exquisite beauty. No literature rivals the Bible's picturesque and simple beauty, its immortal lines of sublime truth.

Jesus painted word pictures that, though unwritten for years, were so unforgettable as to become recorded for all time in *The Greatest Story Ever Told.*

J.B. Phillips, who has given us his striking translation of the New Testament, shares his philosophy: "If . . . words are to enter men's hearts and bear fruit, they must be the right words shaped cunningly to pass men's defenses and explode silently and effectually within their minds."

This proverb speaks to us of the impulse to move beyond necessities toward something called beauty, which is further refined into art. We are not merely a mechanism designed to function efficiently. We have the capacity to imagine and create, as endowed by our imaginative Creator. God delights in beauty as evidenced by the way He shaped and colored fish, birds, insects, and plants with such incredible variety.

The superlative message we have to share deserves the most beautiful adornment. Our proclamation of the sublime must not be allowed to be prosaic. No words can ever be adequate, but the message deserves our painstaking best, our "utmost for His highest."

Word Incarnate, teach me the art of creative expression and to clothe in royal robes of beauty my witness of eternal truths.

FIFTY-FOUR
GOOD NEWS FROM A DISTANT LAND

Like cold water to a weary soul
is good news from a distant land (25:25).

There has been an enforced separation from loved ones. Anxiety crowds the mind over their safety and welfare. A long time has elapsed since word has been received from or of them. Then one day comes the surprise and joy of a letter. It brings the "good news from a distant land" that has been long awaited. It cheers the heart. It refreshes, restores, as that drink of cold water.

The Gospel, above all else, is good news from a distant land. It comes from heaven to earth, from God to man. It is to the thirsty soul the most satisfying drink. It satisfies the deep thirst that no earthly spring can quench. When weary of the journey, we drink its life-giving waters and are refreshed, restored, and enabled to go on.

The story is told of a woman who had an unusual dream of a room full of people, all of them sad and crying. In her dream she knew they were sad because they lived and died feeling they had failed in life.

Suddenly the door of the room opened and in walked Jesus. Seeing the people in distress, He was moved with compassion and began walking about the room, standing in front of each person in turn.

"Why are you crying?" He asked the first one. "I'm

crying, Lord, because our little child died and from then on we were lost without him. I was too distressed all the years after to do anything worthwhile with my life."

"Didn't you get my letter?" He asked, His voice heavy with concern.

"What letter, Lord? Did You write me a letter?"

"Yes, I told you I would not leave you comfortless, but the Holy Spirit would come and give comfort and strength to go on."

The woman looked surprised. "You know," she said, "the minister read those words at the funeral, but I didn't know it was from You to me. If I had only known."

Then Jesus stepped over to the next person in the room. He asked, "Why are you crying?"

The man replied, "Lord, I couldn't live for You because my life was so full of worry and crowded with more things than I could handle."

"Then you didn't get my letter either?" He asked.

"No, Lord," he said. "Did You write me a letter?"

"Yes, and in it I told you about the peace that passes understanding. I told you to seek the kingdom of God and all other essential things would be yours."

"Lord, I do remember reading about that, but I didn't know it was Your letter to me."

He went to each person in the room and for every need there had been words of help and healing in Scripture. But no one had taken them to heart as intended for them personally.

You and I have good news—the best news of all, from a distant land—the most distant land of all. It comes to us from our dearest Friend, who loves us and has done more for us than any other. Let's read the love letters He has sent us!

Loving Lord, lead me this day to someone to be the bearer of the good news from a distant land.

FIFTY-FIVE

TOMORROW IS ALWAYS A DAY AWAY

Do not boast about tomorrow, for you do not know what a day may bring forth (27:1).

A Spanish proverb warns "the road of by and by leads to the house of never-never." One of the best known proverbs (27:1) reminds us that we must not speak or plan as if we have full control of our destinies.

The Epistle of James, sometimes called "the Proverbs of the New Testament," gives similar advice: "Now listen, you who say, 'Today or tomorrow we will go to this or that city, spend a year there, carry on business and make money.' Why, you do not even know what will happen tomorrow" (4:13-14).

Mankind has accumulated an awesome knowledge. We can split atoms, program computers, explore outer space, implant artificial hearts. But when it comes to tomorrow, our knowledge plunges to zero. Many have awakened to find sickness, tragedy, death, war, or perhaps an answer to prayer.

The counterpart of this truth is that it is today that counts. This proverb gives an antidote against presumption and procrastination. God has given us this day. Now is our moment for rising up to our opportunities and fulfilling the obligations of life.

Procrastination and presumptions about the future are

perhaps nowhere more widespread and tragic than in the matter of receiving Christ as Savior and Lord. The trite saying is nevertheless true that "the road to hell is paved with good intentions."

H.A. Ironside gave five reasons why one should not delay coming to Christ. (1) Every day spent in sin is a day lost. Those who are saved always regret not having turned to the Lord earlier. (2) Every day delayed adds to the terrible things you can never undo. (3) God may cease to speak to you any longer by His Holy Spirit because of the hardening of your heart. (4) Death may claim you for his prey. (5) The Lord Jesus Christ may return before you make yourself ready.[46]

"Now," urges the Apostle Paul, "is the accepted time; behold, now is the day of salvation" (2 Cor. 6:2, KJV).

In his poem "Tomorrow," Edgar A. Guest warns of the danger of procrastination:

> He was going to be all that a mortal could be —
> Tomorrow;
> No one should be kinder nor braver than he —
> Tomorrow;
> A friend who was troubled and weary he knew
> Who'd be glad of a lift and who needed it too;
> On him he would call and see what he could do —
> Tomorrow.
> The greatest of workers this man would have been —
> Tomorrow;
> The world would have known him had he ever
> seen — Tomorrow;
> But the fact is he died and faded from view,
> And all that he left here when living was through
> Was a mountain of things he intended to do —
> Tomorrow.[47]

Lord, I accept with gratitude Your precious gift to me of today. Help me live it joyfully and purposefully.

FIFTY-SIX
AVOID SELF-ADVERTISEMENT

Let another praise you, and not your own mouth;
someone else, and not your own lips (27:2).

Are you tempted to tell others about your achievements, abilities, good qualities? Once again excellent counsel streams from this almost 3,000-year-old book.

The person specializing in self-advertisement and self-recommendation becomes boring and obnoxious. He demeans whatever status he happens to possess.

The wise man's strength is attested by his silence and reticence in speaking about himself. He does not seek to manipulate or manufacture praise. He is genuinely surprised when applauded. He is not upset when he does not get a pat on the back, for he is not working for men's praises, but for the glory of God.

William Carey was one of the greatest missionaries and linguists in the history of the church. He translated parts of the Bible into no fewer than thirty-four Indian languages. He began life as a cobbler and kept in front of his cobbler's bench a map of the world, reflecting his yearning to take Christ to those who had not heard of Him. When he arrived in India, many treated him with contempt. Once at a dinner party, a cynic, with the idea of humiliating him, said in a tone that everyone could hear, "I hear, Mr. Carey, you once worked as a shoemaker."

"No, your lordship," answered Carey, "not a shoemaker, only a cobbler." He did not even claim to make shoes, only to mend them.

The Apostle Paul, in his peerless love chapter, tells Christians not to be inflated with their own importance. Christian love, he says, is "neither anxious to impress nor does it cherish inflated ideas of its own importance" (1 Cor. 13:5, PH).

One of the shortest biographies in Scripture is that of Diotrephes, of whom it is written, "Diotrephes, who loves to be first" (3 John 9). Because he put himself first we never hear any more of him. He put himself first, but no one else did, including God. Our Lord reminds us that "many who are first will be last, and many who are last will be first" (Matt. 19:30).

Proverbs' "wisdom to live by" has been confirmed and amplified in the sublime teachings of the New Testament. God's standards of life are unchanging through the centuries. Let us all be His wise and humble cobblers, seeking only His glory.

Eternal God, help me have a heart at leisure from itself, to be averse to self-seeking, humble in self-estimate, and modest in speech.

FIFTY-SEVEN

THE WISE FOOLISH MAN

I am the most ignorant of men (30:2).

Meet the most stupid man of the Bible! He is so by his own admission: "Surely I am more stupid than any man" (30:2, NKJV).

However, ironically, the translation quoted captions this chapter, "The Wisdom of Agur." Which is it? Is he stupid, or wise?

No other record of Agur exists, but his name is forever memorialized by this great chapter he has given us.

We are reminded that a wise man is aware of his ignorance. All our knowledge is as a tiny pebble on an illimitable shore. The reflective person knows that our planet is but a tiny island in an infinite ocean of mystery in the universe.

But Agur knows, as must all men, that although he can never fathom the inscrutable mysteries, there is a God whom he can trust. He refers to God fourteen times, by name or pronoun, in his theological section (30:2-9). His faith in God forms the solid foundation upon which he builds his practical maxims for life.

He asks five rhetorical questions in verse four. His first question, "Who has gone up to heaven and come down?" was answered by Christ: "No one has ever gone into heaven except the One who came from heaven – the Son of Man" (John 3:13). The Apostle Paul adds, "He who descended is also the very One who ascended higher than all the heavens" (Eph. 4:10).

Agur's wisdom is further witnessed by his testimony of the impeccable authority of God's Word: "Every word of God is flawless: He is a shield to those who take refuge in Him" (Prov. 30:5).

Next we will study more wise sayings from this "most ignorant of men"!

"Dear Lord and Father of mankind, forgive my foolish ways" and teach me Your ways and wisdom.

FIFTY-EIGHT

AGUR'S TWO REQUESTS FOR LIFE

Two things I ask of you, O Lord;
do not refuse me before I die (30:7).

Agur, being the simple man he admits to being in his opening lines, makes but two requests of God: "Keep falsehood and lies from me; give me neither poverty nor riches, but give me only my daily bread" (30:8).

He places the highest value upon truth and prays that he will never lie. Commitment to truth and avoidance of falsehood is one of the greatest needs and disciplines of the spiritual life. Truth can be so subtly avoided and compromised, without awareness of duplicity.

It is not easy to know and accept the truth, especially about ourselves. Winston Churchill said, "Every now and then someone will bump into the truth. Usually, he picks himself up and goes on."

May we in our praying be as wise as Agur and ask God to help us never lie.

The second request of Agur is that he might have just the necessities of life, no more, no less. Thus, as he observes, he will avoid the dangers of prosperity and the desperations of poverty. His petition anticipates our Lord's prayer: "Give us this day our daily bread."

Thomas à Kempis, in his monumental fifteenth-century writing, *The Imitation of Christ,* cites simplicity as one of the two great secrets of the Christian's devotion: "By two wings is man lifted above earthly things, even by simplicity and purity. Simplicity ought to be in the intention, purity in the affection. Simplicity reacheth toward God, purity apprehendeth Him and tasteth Him." From our obsession with possessions, Agur of Proverbs, and his kindred spirit à Kempis call us back to the simplicities of life.

Abraham Cowley, writing in the seventeenth century, also expressed his desire for the simple, yet beautiful things of life:

> Ah yet, ere I descend to the grave,
> May I a small house and a large garden have,
> And a few friends, and many books, both true,
> Both wise, and both delightful too!

Help me, Lord, like wise Agur of old, be kept from falsehood and be satisfied with life's essentials and simplicities.

FIFTY-NINE

THE NUMERICAL PROVERBS

There are three things that are too amazing for me,
four that I do not understand (30:18).

This chapter is comprised mostly of what are known as the numerical proverbs. A numerical proverb is introduced by a number reference. Seven groups of numerical proverbs occur in chapter 30, given by Agur.

Agur cites four things that speak to us of insatiable cravings. "There are three things that are never satisfied, four that never say, 'Enough!': the grave, the barren womb, land, which is never satisfied with water, and fire, which never says, 'Enough!' " (30:15-16).

In his next list, he writes in awe of that which is beyond his understanding, reminding us that our world teems with amazing wonders: "There are three things that are too amazing for me, four that I do not understand: the way of an eagle in the sky, the way of a snake on a rock, the way of a ship on the high seas, and the way of a man with a maiden" (30:18-19).

There are four things our author considers unbearable: "Under three things the earth trembles, under four it cannot bear up: a servant who becomes king, a fool who is full of food, an unloved woman who is married, and a maidservant who displaces her mistress" (30:21-23).

All are examples of people out of place and out of tune

with life. We find their counterparts all around us today. There are the undeserving who rise to authority and power, the foolish glutton, the spurned wife, and the person in a privileged position of service who replaces the wife (the "maidservant" today has sometimes become the secretary, the work associate, etc.). A spouse must beware of unholy familiarity that can become domestic fatality. Life still "cannot bear up" under these conditions.

An intriguing list of four little wise things now becomes immortalized by Agur's perceptive presentation: "Four things on earth are small, yet they are extremely wise: Ants are creatures of little strength, yet they store up their food in the summer; conies [badgers] are creatures of little power, yet they make their home in the crags; locusts have no king, yet they advance together in ranks; a spider can be caught with the hand, yet it is found in kings' palaces" (30:24-28).

Agur was almost three millennia ahead of his time! He who saw greatness and wisdom in small things would probably feel right at home in the atomic age where scientists have turned their attention to the microscopic to unravel the mysteries of the universe.

There are many little things of life all around us, invested with the wisdom of the Creator, if we will only reflect upon them.

These numerical proverbs end on the high note of four stately things: "a lion, mighty among beasts, who retreats before nothing; a strutting rooster, a he-goat, and a king with his army around him" (30:30-31).

Do you want to join the company of the stately? The man or woman of God can also stand tall and walk stately through life because his confidence is in God.

Christ the Truth, I enroll as a life student in the school of the Spirit, that He may open my eyes and help me see the wonders and lessons of life all about me.

SIXTY

SPEAK UP FOR THE DESTITUTE

Speak up for all those who cannot speak for themselves, for the rights of all who are destitute (31:8).

The final chapter of Proverbs offers appropriate instruction on two great institutions—the nation and the home.

The first section features counsel to Lemuel as a king. He is warned against lust (31:3) which has been the ruin of mighty men. Strong drink is another cause of downfall to be avoided (31:4-7). He who would rule over a nation must first master himself.

Then his mother appeals for him to help the afflicted and needy: "Speak up for all those who cannot speak for themselves, for the rights of all who are destitute." Never has this mandate to leadership been more urgent. Millions today in our world fit this description—the poor, the oppressed, the refugee, the starving, the abused, the unborn.

This appeal to "speak up for those who cannot speak for themselves" should challenge and galvanize us to speak up for the 1.5 million unborn in this country who are victims of abortion every year. They cannot speak up for themselves. Will we speak up for them? Will we have the courage and conviction to halt this silent holocaust taking place all around us?

The Salvation Army's national publication, *The War*

Cry, has consistently addressed the issues of our time with strong conviction. Theme editions with hard-hitting editorials and documentaries have been published on such issues as abortion, pornography, television violence, drunk driving, immorality, homelessness and hunger, family disintegration, and other current issues that affect the lives of people and our nation.

Such theme editions in the national magazine not only give a diagnosis of the problem but a call to practical action. *The War Cry* has not merely indulged in polemics but gives leadership for concrete action that can make a difference.

This fact is illustrated by the experience of the author, who was guest speaker at a northern California series of camp meetings. While I was walking on the camp-grounds, a young woman greeted me and asked, "Are you the editor?" I replied, "Yes, I am." She further asked, "Do you send out the *War Cry?*" I said, "Yes, I do." Then she pointed to a beautiful baby, less than a year old, in a stroller and said, "She is here because of your *War Cry.*" She then related her story: Pregnant, unmarried, counseled by family and friends to have an abortion, she decided to have an abortion. "Then I read your *War Cry,*" she said, "and that changed my mind. My little girl is here today because of *The War Cry.*" She was referring to a special theme issue on "Alternatives to Abortion." Needless to say, that became a hallowed spot for me, the editor-in-chief.

The responsible Christian is engaged in the business of making a difference, a difference for God in the lives of people as they confront the vital issues of life.

Christ, who championed the cause of the afflicted, help me be a faithful and courageous voice for those who need my encouragement and advocacy.

147

SIXTY-ONE

PORTRAIT OF THE IDEAL WIFE

A wife of noble character who can find?
She is worth far more than rubies (31:10).

This magnificent Book of Proverbs concludes and climaxes with its immortal tribute to the virtuous wife, and the praiseworthy character of her life and deeds.

After many words said about contentious, adulterous, and sinful women, the Book of Proverbs presents this beautiful portrait of wifely excellence.

This eulogy of a noble wife was written in the form of an acrostic in the original Hebrew language. The first letter of each of its twenty-two couplets follows the order of the Hebrew alphabet. That device aided memorization and suggested that the writer had to summon the whole alphabet to describe the virtuous wife. Crawford Toy calls this section the "golden ABCs of the perfect wife."[48]

The virtuous wife is portrayed in her various roles. She is the faithful wife, the diligent mother, the believer known for her reverence of the Lord, her industry and prudence in looking after the needs of her household. Her works are known beyond her own home as she "extends her hands to the needy" (31:20).

Her crowning characteristics are strength, honor, dignity, wisdom, kindness, faith. Her comeliness of soul and mind excel even beauty of face and form. The highest praise proceeds from those who know her best—"her children arise and call her blessed," and her husband exclaims, "you surpass them all" (31:28-29).

This praise of the noble wife is so superlative that we must include selected verses from the text without further comment.

> A wife of noble character who can find?
>   She is worth far more than rubies.
> Her husband has full confidence in her
>   and lacks nothing of value.
> She brings him good, not harm,
>   all the days of her life.
> She selects wool and flax
>   and works with eager hands.
> She considers a field and buys it;
>   out of her earnings she plants a vineyard.
> She sets about her work vigorously;
>   her arms are strong for her tasks.
> She sees that her trading is profitable,
>   and her lamp does not go out at night.
> She opens her arms to the poor
>   and extends her hands to the needy.
> When it snows, she has no fear for her household;
>   for all of them are clothed in scarlet.
> She is clothed with strength and dignity;
>   she can laugh at the days to come.
> She speaks with wisdom,
>   and faithful instruction is on her tongue.
> She watches over the affairs of her household
>   and does not eat the bread of idleness.
> Her children arise and call her blessed,
>   her husband also, and he praises her:
> "Many women do noble things,
>   but you surpass them all."
> Charm is deceptive, and beauty is fleeting;
>   but a woman who fears the Lord is to be praised.

149

Give her the reward she has earned,
and let her works bring her praise at the city gate.

The Book of Proverbs, that puts religion in working clothes and relates it to our world of practical relationships and realities, could not end on a higher note!

Lord, for the devotion and virtue of those who love me, I thank You. Help me be true for those who trust me, pure for those who care, and more worthy of their love.

150

SIXTY-TWO
ONE GREATER THAN SOLOMON

*Now one greater than Solomon is here
(Matthew 12:42).*

What could someone living 3,000 years ago have to say to our day? How could a person who never traveled more than 25 miles an hour (in a chariot), or farther than several hundred miles, relate to our time of supersonic speed and mind-boggling space travel? Surely such a person's thoughts would be obsolete to the business of everyday life in our modern world.

Yet, as we have seen in our meditations from the Book of Proverbs, this ancient book is as up-to-date as tomorrow's newscast. A man traveling at 700 miles an hour can struggle with the problems addressed in Proverbs just as easily as at 25 miles an hour. Modern technology can leave us bankrupt in wisdom for living; it cannot show us how to improve the conduct and character of life.

The timeless truths and teachings of Proverbs still present God's blueprint for character and conduct. We need its vertical wisdom for our horizontal living.

Jesus, referred to the Queen of Sheba "who came from the ends of the earth to listen to Solomon's wisdom," and added, "Now one greater than Solomon is here" (Matt. 12:42).

In our quest for wisdom, we must move beyond the

sage of this book to "One greater than Solomon," He who is Wisdom Incarnate, who is our ultimate Teacher and Example.

A young, proud man captained his ship on the high seas. He spied two lights in the distance and ordered his radio man to transmit a message across the seas: "Alter your course ten degrees south." An answer radioed back, "Alter your course ten degrees north."

The indignant captain ordered the response back across the high seas: "You alter your course ten degrees south—this is Captain Martin." The answer demanded yet another time, "You alter your course ten degrees north—this is Seaman Third-class Bailey."

The irate captain fired again: "You alter your course ten degrees south—I am a battleship and I am coming through." Seaman Bailey radioed one last time, "I am a lighthouse and I am not going to move!"

Many in life proudly follow their own course, arrogantly making their theme song, "I'll do it my way." Only when we steer life's course according to the Light of the World will we avoid shipwreck upon the treacherous rocks and shoals about us. The wisdom of the ages is found alone in the One greater than Solomon and all the sages who ever lived.

Paul the Apostle proclaimed the message of "Christ, in whom are hidden all the treasures of wisdom and knowledge" (Col. 2:2-3). Let us then, with Proverbs' wisdom as a foundation, build our lives on the supreme wisdom of Christ, who does not merely impart wisdom, but Himself is Divine Wisdom. He will bestow the highest benefit, beauty, and blessing upon our path of life.

"Send out Your light and Your truth; Lord, into my heart let them shine," that my life may reflect the beauty of Your holiness.

Section Two

Words of Wisdom
from Ecclesiastes

SIXTY-THREE

THE STRANGEST BOOK IN THE BIBLE

The words of the Teacher (1:1).

Ecclesiastes has been called the strangest book in the Bible. It portrays the Creator as impersonal and inscrutable. Its mood is one of disillusionment, doubt, and melancholy. Its pessimistic eloquence is unmatched in Scripture.

Even the Song of Songs, which with its erotic tone may seem out of place in the Bible, can be interpreted as an allegory of God's love for Israel. But no such option exists for this book.

If Ecclesiastes is the strangest, it is also one of the most fascinating books of the Bible. Its poetic and philosophic eloquence has carved it a place among the great literature of the world. Renowned Bible scholar Franz Delitzsch calls it "the quintessence of piety."

Derek Kidner describes the writer of Ecclesiastes as an explorer whose "concern is with the boundaries of life, and especially with the questions that most of us would hesitate to push too far. His probing is so relentless that he can easily be taken for a skeptic or a pessimist."[1] The writer of this book takes us on an odyssey of the spirit that requires courage to face life's brevity and seeming futility.

His reflections and soliloquies probe some of our deepest doubts and questions. "No book in the Old Testament," states the *Interpreter's Bible,* "so challenges Christian faith to meet the questions it asks, questions as old as our human perplexities, as old as our search for the meaning of life. . . . No book in the Old Testament faces vaster frontiers."[2]

We will find as we journey with the Teacher that he does not bring us back empty-handed. The serious reader will go beyond the book's dark and disconsolate passsages and discover at the end its lamp of truth shining all the brighter because of the darkness from which we emerge. The reader will gain courage from the hard-won affirmation at the book's climax. Too many fail to venture beyond its portals of "vanity of vanities" to reach its "conclusion of the matter."

Alexander Pope penned lines which echo the Teacher's philosophy:

> The proper study of mankind is Man . . .
> Born to die; and reasoning but to err;
> . . . in endless error hurled:
> The glory, jest, and riddle of the world![3]

Fasten your spiritual seatbelt for this adventurous search to exciting frontiers of the spiritual realm!

Christ, the Pioneer of our faith, lead me on a journey of self-discovery and a closer walk with You.

SIXTY-FOUR

KNOW THYSELF

Son of David, king in Jerusalem (1:1).

The Greeks had inscribed the words "Know thyself" above the temple of the oracle at Delphi. Knowing the meaning of life is the great quest of Ecclesiastes. It poses the quintessential questions: Who am I? Where did I come from? Why am I here? Where am I going? It probes relentlessly and is at times a devastating and unsettling search. It delivers us from any self-confident or rose-colored world view.

The greatest study of all is not astronomy, archeology, geology, zoology, or biology. The highest knowledge to attain is that of mankind himself and his relation to God. The dictum of Socrates and the Greeks, "Know thyself," is what the Book of Ecclesiastes is all about.

The title *Ecclesiastes* comes from the opening phrase, "The words of the Teacher" (1:1). The Hebrew word for "Teacher" is "goheleth," which in Greek is "Ecclesiastes." "Teacher" or "preacher" are the common English translations of the term.

The author is not named but is cryptically identified as the "son of David, king in Jerusalem." Tradition favors Solomon, the patron of wisdom in Israel, as the author, based on this statement and supported by internal references: the author's unrivaled wisdom (1:16), his wealth (2:8), his extensive building projects (2:4-6) and his collection of proverbs (12:9). Solomon, of course, fits all these roles.

Solomon's quest in this book shows the futility of pursuing earthly goals as an end in themselves, and would lead us to God as the only source of fulfillment. Solomon himself became the classic example of folly when he started to live according to his own script instead of God's. His "all-you-can-eat lifestyle" eventually led to fatal heartburn. When he forsook the wisdom of God, he became the wisest fool who ever ruled.

Jim Elliot wrote before his death as a missionary martyr: "He is no fool who gives what he cannot keep to gain what he cannot lose." May we ever live by that kind of heavenly wisdom.

God, who knows me utterly, lead me to a deeper understanding of myself and Your wisdom for me.

158

SIXTY-FIVE
THE VICIOUS CIRCLE

"Meaningless! Meaningless!" says the Teacher.
"Utterly meaningless!
Everything is meaningless!" (1:2).

This is probably the most despondent and pessimistic opening of any piece of literature. "Vanity" says one translator. "A wisp of vapor" says another. "A puff of wind" writes a third. Solomon describes the sum of life itself!

As one of the most creative writers of the Bible, he employs two strategies for effectiveness. He opens with the arresting element of surprise. Who would have expected a preacher to commence with such a declaration of futility? It creates a shock effect. He also employs repetition. The word translated "meaningless" or "vanity" appears thirty-three times in this brief book. He is not being redundant; he is underscoring his finding that life is meaningless.

"The mass of men lead lives of quiet desperation," announced Henry David Thoreau of his generation. The son of David found it so in his lifetime. It is a dominant characteristic of our world. Many find life to be grinding boredom, futile, and purposeless.

His famous phrase "under the sun" (1:3) occurs thirty times, providing a key phrase and clue to this book. Right at the start this phrase reminds us that the writer is deal-

159

ing from an earthbound horizon. His observations originate from ground level. His statements are limited to the seen world. The vertical perspective is not found until the end, and is not complete until we come to the New Testament.

The writer cites the ceaseless cycles of nature as proof of the vicious circle of life. The wearisome repetition is seen in the generations that come and go (1:4), the rising and setting of the sun (1:5), the circular currents of the wind (1:6), the flow of waters in their channels (1:7), and the repetitive boredom of all things (1:8).

The writer defines history as a closed circuit with his famous phrase "nothing new under the sun" (1:9-10). True, our world is not as static as his, but the change and novelty are in externals. Man, in his nature and needs, remains the same. He further laments we will all be forgotten as will our children after us (1:11).

How does all this square with our outlook on life? Is it all a vicious circle? A treadmill of activity? A routine that brings tedium? Or "a chasing after the wind" in the repeated metaphor of the Teacher (1:17; 2:11, 18, 26)? Or have we found something better?

Heavenly Father, open my eyes to see dawn beyond dusk, sunshine above shadows and the Light of the World amid the darkness around me.

SIXTY-SIX

DEAD-END PATHS

*Yet when I surveyed all that my hands had done
and what I had toiled to achieve,
everything was meaningless, a chasing after the wind;
nothing was gained under the sun (2:11).*

The teacher looks to wisdom in his search for meaning:
"I devoted myself to study and to explore by wisdom all
that is done under heaven" (1:13). But he finds "with
much wisdom comes much sorrow" (1:18). Science
always raises more questions than it answers. Our larger
telescopes only add incalculable light-years to the mysteries of the universe, leaving man more humbled before
the God of stars and nebulae, which are but the trailing of
His garments.

He next searches for meaning by tasting life's pleasures
to the fullest (2:1). He then looks for it in laughter (2:2).
He becomes a connoisseur of the choicest wines (2:3).
He erects great buildings—his palace (2:4). He plants
vineyards, designs beautiful parks and luxurious gardens
(2:5-6). He employs an astonishing number of people. His
herds of livestock would make the Guinness record book
of his day (2:7). His wealth was legendary (2:8). As a
patron of the arts, he enjoyed the best music (2:8). His
harem of 700 wives and 300 concubines would prompt
Henry VIII to blush with envy. He writes the script for
"wine, women, and song."

And where did this impassioned quest for pleasure and

possessions lead him? What was the result of all his brilliant achievements, the realization of his highest ambitions? After surveying all his pleasures and accomplishments, he pronounces his verdict:

> I denied myself nothing my eyes desired;
> I refused my heart no pleasure. . . .
> Yet when I surveyed all that my hands had done and
> what I toiled to achieve,
> everything was meaningless, a chasing after the wind;
> nothing was gained under the sun (2:10-11).

The king's gardens have become dust and windblown down the corridors of time, but the lesson remains. Many today still search these same roads for meaning in life. They look for fulfillment in knowledge, pleasures, fun and laughter, alcohol and drugs, work, possessions, aesthetics and the arts.

The deep needs and desires of our souls can never be satisfied with the things of earth. This classic book will lead us further in our search for meaning.

> *Spirit of eternal love,*
> *Guide me, or I blindly rove;*
> *set my heart on things above,*
> *Draw me after Thee.*
> *Earthly things are paltry show,*
> *Phantom charms, they come and go;*
> *Give me constantly to know*
> *Fellowship with Thee.*[4]

SIXTY-SEVEN
IS THAT ALL THERE IS?

*I hated life. . . . All of it is meaningless,
a chasing after the wind (2:17).*

We left the Teacher in the last chapter "in the pits." All his pursuits for meaning ended with his verdict of "meaningless." As we read on he acknowledges death as the great leveler for the wise man and the fool (2:14-16).

He laments: "I hated all the things I had toiled for under the sun, because I must leave them to the one who comes after me. And who knows whether he will be a wise man or a fool? Yet he will have control over all the work in which I have poured my effort and skill under the sun" (2:18-19).

Every diligent workman must identify with his concern. Will posterity appreciate or repudiate the values by which dedicated and diligent work provided a legacy? Will blessings be taken for granted which an earlier generation struggled to provide? From his vantage point of "under the sun," he pronounces life to be "meaningless."

One can almost hear Peggy Lee's doleful tones, "Is that all . . . is that all there is?" blowing across the dirge-like lament of these pages. Is that all there is to knowledge? Is that all there is to pleasures? Is that all there is to wealth? Is that all there is to wine? Is that all there is to building projects? Is that all there is to possessions? Is that all there is to sex? Is that all there is to aesthetics?

But now a shaft of light falls on his path of darkness. He has to acknowledge that "satisfaction . . . is from the hand of God, for without Him who can . . . find enjoyment?" (2:24-25). God alone is the source of true wisdom and happiness (2:26). It is a major breakthrough in his search for meaning.

Many modern-day believers echo this truth in the words of the old hymn whose author is known only as "B.E.":

> O Christ, in Thee my soul hath found,
> And found in Thee alone,
> The peace, the joy, I sought so long,
> The bliss till now unknown.
>
> I tried the broken cisterns, Lord,
> But, ah! the waters failed;
> E'en as I stopped to drink they fled,
> And mocked me as I wailed.
>
> Now none but Christ can satisfy,
> No other name for me;
> There's love and life and lasting joy,
> Lord Jesus, found in Thee.

In the stillness of this moment, Lord, come and infuse my life with Your wisdom and love.

SIXTY-EIGHT

WHAT TIME IS IT?

There is a time for everything,
and a season for every activity under heaven (3:1).

In one of the better-known poetic portions of Scripture, fourteen couplets cover the range of human activity:

> *a time to be born and a time to die,*
> *a time to plant and a time to uproot,*
> *a time to kill and a time to heal,*
> *a time to tear down and a time to build,*
> *a time to weep and a time to laugh,*
> *a time to mourn and a time to dance,*
> *a time to scatter stones and a time to gather them,*
> *a time to embrace and a time to refrain,*
> *a time to search and a time to give up,*
> *a time to keep and a time to throw away,*
> *a time to tear and a time to mend,*
> *a time to be silent and a time to speak,*
> *a time to love and a time to hate,*
> *a time for war and a time for peace (3:2-8).*

The Teacher starts with the most momentous events of birth and death, the two parameters that surround our lives. He seems to suggest the tyranny of time with his rhythmic and monotonous repetition—"a time to. . . ."

"A time to plant and . . . uproot" reminds us we must cooperate with the seasons of life. Each time or experience has its antithesis, its opposite—kill and heal, tear down and build, weep and laugh, mourn and dance, etc. The tapestry of life is woven from such contrasts, and these contrasts give it meaning and beauty.

One backwoods woman wrote a complaint to the government about the newfangled daylight savings time, saying "That extra hour of sunshine done burnt up all my tomato plants." There is the danger of looking at time as an enemy rather than a friend. It often depends on the perspective we bring to it.

"Time and tide wait for no man." Time is opportunity. Like the tide, it comes in for a brief moment and then is gone. Shakespeare's Brutus urges us not to lose life's ventures and be left in the shallows:

> There is a tide in the affairs of men
> Which, taken at the flood, leads on to fortune;
> Omitted, all the voyage of their life
> Is bound in shallows and in miseries.
> On such a full sea are we now afloat;
> And we must take the current when it serves
> Or lose our ventures.

Thomas Chalmers once said, "Mathematician that I was, I had forgotten two magnitudes—the shortness of time and the vastness of eternity." May we ever have that kind of binocular perception of God's precious gift to us of time.

There is no present like time! Let us invest it wisely to reap its rich and rewarding dividends.

May we, Lord, with the psalmist pray, "My times are in Your hands" (31:15)

WHAT AM I WORKING FOR?

What does the worker gain from his toil? (3:9)

The questions of Ecclesiastes continue with unsparing assessment of the essential things of life. The Teacher now probes, "What does the worker gain from his toil?"

This question stops us in the midst of our frantic activity, our hurried pace, our preoccupation with our tasks. It makes us ask, "What is the value of it all?" "What am I working for?" "Who am I working for?" "What does it all matter?"

Our toil in life should be for something more than earthly wages. Something more than man's praises or plaudits. Something more than material success. The precepts of these books of wisdom would lead us to a theology of work—its purpose and principles. In the end, the highest reward for a man's toil is not what he gets for it, but rather what he becomes by it.

A parable, shared by the late Peter Marshall, offers a perspective on the meaning of life and work:

> Once upon a time, a certain town grew up at the foot of a mountain range. High up in the hills, a quiet forest dweller took it upon himself to be the Keeper of the Springs. He patrolled the hills, and wherever

he found a spring, he cleaned its brown pool of silt and fallen leaves, of mud and mold, and took away from the spring all foreign matter, so that the water which bubbled up through the sand ran down clean and cold and pure.

It leaped sparkling over rocks and dropped joyously in crystal cascades until, swollen by other streams, it became a river of life to the busy town.

Millwheels were whirled by its rush. Gardens were refreshed by its waters. Fountains threw it like diamonds into the air. Swans sailed upon its limpid surface, and children laughed as they played on its banks in the sunshine.

But, the City Council was a group of hard-headed, hard-boiled businessmen. They scanned the civic budget and found in it the salary of a Keeper of the Springs. Said the Keeper of the Purse: "Why should we pay this romance ranger? We never see him; he is not necessary to our town's work life. If we build a reservoir just above the town, we can dispense with his services and save his salary." Therefore, the City Council voted to dispense with the unnecessary cost of a Keeper of the Springs and to build a cement reservoir.

When it was finished, it soon filled with water, to be sure, but the water did not seem to be the same. It did not seem to be as clean, and a green scum soon befouled its stagnant surface. The delicate machinery of the mills became clogged with slime and the swans found another home above the town. At last, an epidemic raged, and the clammy, yellow fingers of sickness reached into every home in every street and lane.

The City Council met again. Sorrowfully, it faced the city's plight, and frankly acknowledged the mistake of the dismissal of the Keeper of the Spring. They sought him out in his hermit hut high in the hills, and begged him to return to his former joyous labor. Gladly he agreed and began once more to make his rounds.

It was not long until pure water came lilting down under tunnels of ferns and mosses to sparkle in the cleansed reservoir. Millwheels turned again as of old. Stenches disappeared. Sickness waned and convalescent children playing in the sun laughed again because the swans had come back.[5]

There never has been a time when there has been a greater need for Keepers of the Springs — in our communities, in our families, and in our individual lives. Pollutants from many sources threaten to destroy the purity, the refreshing wholesomeness, the sustaining sources of life. Violence and sexploitation have invaded our very living rooms through merchants of menace and the purveyors of perversion in the television industry. The moral cancer of pornography is eating at the heart of America.

There is work God has for all of us to do. Let us go forth, in our homes, communities, country, and the world, and be His keepers of the springs.

Lord, help me have a vulnerable involvement amid the hurts and heartaches, the corruption, and chaos of our world.

SEVENTY
HIS TOUCH OF BEAUTY

He has made everything beautiful in its time (3:11).

The writer now moves into a new focus. There is a mo-
mentary relief from his statement of meaninglessness
and purposelessness. He shifts from his earth-bound horizon of "under the sun" and shares a perspective that
looks beyond the things of earth to God. He gives us one
of the sublime statements of the Bible about God's creative handiwork: "He has made everything beautiful in its
time."

It is mind-boggling to contemplate the beauty and majesty of God's creation. Just think of some wonders He has
endowed us with in such abandonment: stars, flowers,
birds, oceans, lakes, rivers, streams, sunsets, mountains,
trees, fish, animals, rain.

A poet has expressed our response of awe:

One midnight deep in the starlight still
I dreamed that I received this bill—
... in account with life:
Five thousand breathless dawns all new;
Five thousand flowers fresh in dew;
Five thousand sunsets wrapped in gold;
One million snowflakes served ice cold;

170

Five quiet friends; one baby's love;
One white sea with clouds above;
One hundred music-haunted dreams —
  Of moon-drenched roads and hurrying streams,
  Of prophesying winds and trees,
  Of silent stars and drowsing bees,
One June night in a fragrant wood;
One heart that loved and understood!
I wondered when I waked at day
How in God's name, I could pay.
  —Courtland W. Sayres

Our world is one of extravagant beauty and marvelous design. We who live under star-strewn skies, who are greeted each day with the grand spectacle of a sunrise, who walk among the exquisite beauty of flowers and songs of birds in the trees, who know the restless tides of oceans and the towering grandeur of mountains — these and countless wonders all about us — render us fabulously wealthy with endowments of our Creator.

He indeed has made everything beautiful. With the lyricist, Mary Susan Edgar, we would pray:

God, who touchest earth with beauty,
  Make my heart anew;
With Thy Spirit recreate me
  Pure and strong and true.
Like Thy springs and running waters,
  Make me crystal pure;
Like Thy rocks of towering grandeur,
  Make me strong and sure.[6]

171

SEVENTY-ONE

ETERNITY IN OUR HEARTS

He has also set eternity in the hearts of men (3:11).

This text now brings us to one of the unexpected summits of this book. This flowering text stands on its own, apart from its context, as a sovereign mountain peak of truth that dominates the landscape of life.

All around us God has put intimations of our immortality. He has planted within us an unrelenting intuition to see beyond temporal horizons and press beyond the limits of the infinite. A sense of destiny haunts us. Eternal forces ripple in our blood. Immortal cadences echo in our ears. Sublime visions flash upon the screen of our imagination. Eternity beckons as deep calls unto the depths God has put in our souls.

With Francis Thompson, from his haunting *The Hound of Heaven* written almost a century ago, we hear the sound of a distant trumpet:

> Yet ever and anon a trumpet sounds
> From the hid battlements of Eternity.

Augustine summarized this longing and homesickness of the soul: "O God, You have made us for Yourself and our hearts are restless until they find their rest in You."

"Eternity is at our hearts," wrote Thomas Kelly, "pressing upon our time-torn lives, warming us with intimations of an astounding destiny, calling us home unto Itself. Yielding to these persuasions, gladly committing ourselves in body and soul, utterly and completely, to the Light Within, is the beginning of true life."[7]

May we yield to this Light Within who brings radiance and joy and fulfillment.

With Salvationist Bramwell Coles, let us pray:

Dull are my ears to hear Thy voice,
Slow are my hands to work for Thee,
Loath are my feet to conquer the steeps
That lead me to my Calvary.

Strength for my weakness, Lord, impart;
Sight for my blindness give to me;
Faith for my doubtings, Lord, I would crave,
That I may serve Thee worthily.[8]

SEVENTY-TWO

DUST TO DUST

All come from dust, and to dust all return (3:20).

The pessimistic discourse on wickedness and injustice climaxes in words that have been paraphrased innumerable times in the final parting over an open grave: "From dust thou art, to dust return."

The Greek poet Euripides called death "the debt we all must pay." George Bernard Shaw expressed it bluntly: "The statistics on death are quite impressive: One out of one people dies." The invincible reaper knocks ultimately at every door. "Man is destined to die once," declares the writer of Hebrews (9:27). The irreversible fact is that no matter what our diet, how diligently we exercise, how many vitamins and health foods we eat, how low we keep our cholesterol—someday we will die.

According to an old Oriental legend, a wealthy merchant in Baghdad one day sent his servant to the marketplace to obtain provisions for the household. In a little while the servant returned. He came running into the presence of his master, his limbs trembling and his face pale with fright.

"What is wrong?" exclaimed the merchant.

"Master," cried the servant, "I just now met Death in the marketplace, and when Death saw me, he raised his arm to strike me. Master, I am afraid. I must escape. Let me, I pray, borrow your fastest horse, and I shall flee to Samarra."

The merchant, being a kindhearted man, consented, and the servant rode swiftly away to the city of Samarra."

After the servant had departed, the merchant himself took the market basket and went to the marketplace. He too saw Death, and approached him boldly. "Death," he asked, "why did you raise your hand to strike my servant here in the marketplace a little while ago?"

"Why," answered Death, "I meant him no harm—that was a gesture of surprise. I was surprised to see him here in Baghdad, for I have an appointment with him tonight in the city of Samarra."

Death is inevitable. All must die. Every man has an appointment with death. The question is, *Are we ready for death?*

An eternal truth is enshrined in the reply of the little girl who was asked if she was afraid because her path from school led through a graveyard. She replied, "No, I just cross it to reach home."

Let us affirm our faith in the prayer of John Henry Newman:

O Lord, support us all the day long,
until the shadows lengthen and the evening comes,
and the busy world is hushed,
and the fever of life is over, and our work is done.
Then, Lord, in Your mercy grant us a safe lodging,
and a holy rest, and peace at the last;
through Jesus Christ our Lord.

SEVENTY-THREE

A HANDFUL OF QUIETNESS

Better is a handful with quietness than both hands full, together with toil and grasping for the wind (4:6, NKJV).

We are immersed in a world of clamor, crowds, and cacophony. Sound-soaked days and nights in metropolitan areas bombard tenants with the roar of jets, the din of traffic, the scream of sirens, the tumult of voices. The electronic age intrudes upon us by telephone (now portable), television, beepers, and computer telecommunications. A "handful of quietness" has become an "endangered specie."

The royal penman of Ecclesiastes perceived that it was better to have less, a handful with quietness, than to have more, both hands full but consumed with toil and futility. The writer employs two different words for "hand." The second means hands cupped to take as much as possible. Living for possessions, position, perquisites is, as Solomon discovered, "a grasping for the wind." This text powerfully preaches to our culture that thinks *bigger* is better and *more* is most.

For many today, life consists of two handfuls along with toil and futility. The pleasures and perks for which life is spent do not bring deep joy and peace. The outer life is full of many things, but the inner life remains hollow. The missing ingredient is quietness or, as rendered by the

NIV, "tranquility." Inner disquiet impoverishes life in the deepest sense.

We need to get out of the fast lane, to withdraw from the constant erosions of our inner resources. We need to experience solitude, stillness, and serenity. We need moments stripped of life's distracting non-essentials, to get alone to what Thomas Kelly called "the recreating silences." Many today critically need "a handful of quietness."

In one of more than 500 sonnets, William Wordsworth laments the increasing busyness brought on by the Industrial Revolution. His words correspond with the insight of our text:

> The world is too much with us; late and soon,
> Getting and spending, we lay waste our powers;
> Little we see in Nature that is ours;
> We have given our hearts away, a sordid boon! . . .
> We are out of tune.

It is easy to miss the accents of the Eternal in the hustle and bustle of our world. "Be still, and know that I am God" (Ps. 46:10) becomes a text with urgency in our noise-saturated world.

In the Teacher's metaphor, it seems that God has given us two hands so that one can be filled with quietness and tranquility. If both have been filled with the things of the world, perhaps we need to unclasp one of our hands, let go and reach out to take the higher gift God has for us, the gift of peace.

> *Drop Thy still dews of quietness*
> *Till all our strivings cease;*
> *Take from our souls the strain and stress,*
> *And let our ordered lives confess*
> *The beauty of Thy peace.*
> *—John Greenleaf Whittier*

177

SEVENTY-FOUR

THE CORD OF FRIENDSHIP

Two are better than one,
because they have a good return for their work (4:9).

"There was a man all alone" (4:8) intimates what some believe to be the worst of all human afflictions—loneliness. This man is described as having neither friend nor family. His notable achievements do not satisfy.

"Loneliness" has been called the most desolate word in the English language. Ours has become a lonely society; old-fashioned neighborliness has given way to urban high rises and private lifestyles.

We come to one of the beautiful serendipities in Ecclesiastes as the author moves from the despair of loneliness to the blessing of companionship. "Two are better than one" (4:9) he records in his journal. He cites three circumstances of life to illustrate his point.

> If one falls down,
>   his friend can help him up.
> But pity the man who falls
>   and has no one to help him up!
> Also, if two lie down together, they will keep warm.
>   But how can one keep warm alone?
> Though one may be overpowered,
>   two can defend themselves (4:10-12).

Who of us does not have moments of weakness, those times when we stumble and fall, times of failure when we need a friend? What of those "cold" moments in our lives, when the sunshine is obscured by some dark night of loss or distress, and we crave the warmth of a friend's presence? None of us is exempt from hostile attacks — the fierce onslaughts of Satan, the assaults of circumstances, the misunderstanding of others. In such moments, friendship is sustenance, perhaps even survival, as our text suggests.

Add to these the dimension of enrichment that friendship and companionship bring. "A friend may well be reckoned the masterpiece of nature," eulogized Emerson. Coleridge described friendship as a "sheltering tree." The last two lines of Yeats' *A Municipal Gallery Revisited* echoes the theme: "Think where man's glory most begins and ends, / And say my glory was, I had such friends." A great man was once asked the secret of his achievements. He replied, "I had a friend."

Helen Parker, in her poem "Discovery," shares the high worth of friendship given by the Teacher:

> Today a man discovered gold and fame;
> Another flew the stormy seas;
> Another saw an unnamed world aflame;
> One found the germ of disease.
> But what high fates my paths attend:
> For I — today I found a friend.

Our text summarizes this choice discourse on companionship with its powerful metaphor: "A cord of three strands is not quickly broken" (4:12).

The strength of the three-ply cord was proverbial in the ancient world. One cord can easily be broken. Two cords are difficult to break. But three cords cannot be pulled apart.

When husband and wife take the Lord as their third

179

and chief strand, their marriage becomes unbreakable amid the stresses of life.

As children of our Heavenly Father, may we all be bound together by cords of love, and so united, stand triumphant before life's testings and trials.

Thank You, God, for my friends, for the joy and enrichment they bring to my life. Help me live more worthily of their trust and love.

SEVENTY-FIVE

THE JEWEL OF WORSHIP

Stand in awe of God (5:7).

The writer next offers practical and sacred counsel for "when you go to the house of God" (5:1). Worship is far from a passive experience. It has active requirements. Preparation and care are required. The house of God must be reverently entered as cautioned by the words "Guards your steps" (5:1).

"Go near to listen" (5:1) implies the discipline of silence and concentration. True listening is an intellectually aggressive experience. It involves more than ears; it enlists the mind and heart. Because listening is an art and is hard work, most people do it poorly. The writer of Ecclesiastes reminds us of the responsibility to listen when we go to worship.

It is all too easy to go to the house of God with preoccupied minds, lingering tensions, taking with us the tempo of the world around us.

The writer reminds us of the sanctity of vows: "When you make a vow to God, do not delay in fulfilling it." (5:4).

We need to take God seriously and be responsible for our prayers and vows. The last words of Lot's wife may have been, "Why shouldn't we be able to take one last

181

look?" She failed to take God seriously and paid a heavy price. We can't play games with God.

The statement on worship climaxes, "Therefore stand in awe of God" (5:7). Tennyson expressed this sacred privilege of divine communion in memorable verse:

Speak to Him thou for He hears,
   and Spirit with Spirit can meet
Closer is He than breathing,
   and nearer than hands and feet.[9]

"Worship is the missing jewel of the evangelical church," declared A.W. Tozer. There is no nobler task to which we can devote ourselves. May the facets of this jewel scintillate in our personal and corporate experience.

William Temple, late Archbishop of Canterbury, elevates adoration of God to its high and holy place in our lives with his definition of worship:

To Worship
Is to quicken the conscience by the holiness of God,
To feed the mind with the truth of God,
To purge the imagination by the beauty of God,
To open the heart to the love of God,
To devote the will to the purpose of God.

Let us heed the ancient advice of our text when we "go to the house of God" and "therefore stand in awe of God"!

O God, "pavilioned in splendor and girded with praise," help me worship You in reverence and in the beauty of holiness.

SEVENTY-SIX
YOU CAN'T TAKE
IT WITH YOU

Whoever loves money never has money enough;
whoever loves wealth is never satisfied with his income.
This too is meaningless (5:10).

The teacher discourses on money (5:8-17), one of our
most compelling interests. Worse than the addiction it
brings is the emptiness it leaves: "This too," he concludes, "is meaningless."

The axiom "You can't take it with you" may well have
come from, "Naked a man comes from his mother's
womb, and as he comes, so he departs. He takes nothing
from his labor that he can carry in his hand." (5:15). A
Spanish proverb states, "There are no pockets in a
shroud." And no one has ever seen a U-Haul following a
hearse!

"Whoever loves money never has money enough" suggests that the love of money is addictive. When one lives
for money it becomes an obsession. Its pursuit is insatiable. The love of money can control one's life and often
has been the cause of dishonesty and crime. People
think they will be satisfied if they just reach the next
stratum of income or possessions, only to find themselves
obsessed with ambition for the next level.

Seneca the Roman wisely observed that "money has
never yet made anyone rich." True wealth is not mea-
sured in monetary terms. A man or woman is truly

183

wealthy who is rich in loved ones, friends, joy, peace, and purposeful living.

A letter I received from retired Christian leader and friend John D. Waldron reflects the portfolio of a rich man. In response to a request for a writing assignment, he cited some of his commitments to service and added, "And I do need time to saw firewood, spend time with the grandchildren, feed the birds, listen to good music, enjoy the sunrises, shovel snow, feast on my wife's home cooking, help in the local church, read some good books, and in general enjoy the leisurely life of retirement." This man of prodigious achievement, even in retirement years, had a disciplined sense of priorities.

Those who have found life's true values would not take all the wealth on Wall Street in exchange for the non-material riches that bring abiding joy and peace. Jesus gave the key to true happiness in His Beatitudes. Each begins with, "Blessed are" (Matt. 5:3-11). The Greek word *makarios* translated "blessed" literally means "spiritually prosperous [that is, with life-joy and satisfaction in God's favor and salvation, regardless of their outward conditions]" (v. 3, AMP).

No economic condition can deprive us of spiritual prosperity. Such wealth far exceeds the ratings of Dun and Bradstreet. It is not subject to depressions or fluctuations. It is stable and pays fantastic dividends. Let's be among God's plutocrats!

Heavenly Father, You hold in Your hands the wealth of the world; thank You that You have called me to be a child of the King. Help me prize and pursue the true values and riches of Your eternal Kingdom.

SEVENTY-SEVEN

REPUTATION

A good name is better than fine perfume (7:1).

Reputation, of all human possessions, is perhaps the least tangible yet the most zealously guarded. As Shakespeare's foul villain, Iago, puts it in *Othello,* "Good name in man and woman is the immediate jewel of their souls." That is why the right of the aggrieved to seek redress for slander and libel was introduced into English common law during the Middle Ages and survives in U.S. law today.

As long ago as Solomon, "a good name" was of highest worth: "A good name is better than fine perfume" (7:1).

A good name is earned by character and responsibility. May we so live by God's grace that we will merit a good name, which will be more precious than any material assets.

We have seen in recent years how fragile is one's name and reputation. People in high and even holy places have had their good names shattered by compromise and folly. Our nation agonized through the travail of Watergate that should write the epitaph for "situation ethics." A shadow fell across the man who held the highest office in our nation. Chappaquidick has become synonymous with another tainted name of a national leader.

And "Gospelgate" ruined reputations in a series of incredible and scandalous disclosures.

The best and only secure preservative of reputation is one's character and integrity. The fragrance of a good name is more enduring and enhancing than the most costly perfume. Let's not allow any word or deed to rob us of it.

Help me, Lord, to so live with integrity that my reputation will be a witness to Your grace and glory.

SEVENTY-EIGHT

MARRIAGE FIDELITY

Enjoy life with your wife, whom you love (9:9).

Many rich texts are sprinkled throughout this fascinating Book of Ecclesiastes. Regrettably, we must pass many of them by in the interest of space. But the wise counsel above merits our pause and reflection.

Whoever would have thought that having the same wife one started out with would become such a rare experience? Even best-selling Christian writers and effervescent television evangelists have been snared by the divorce-and-second-spouse "sin-drome."

This ancient book sounds a clarion call to marital happiness and fidelity. May we hear and heed its old but up-to-date advice.

For years a tradition was carried on at the famous Church in the Wildwood. Following the wedding ceremony, the minister would say to the bride, "Now pull the bell rope that will ring the bell announcing to the community that your wedding has been performed." The bell was specially rigged so that the bride alone was not strong enough to ring it. The minister would then instruct the groom, "Help her pull it." Their combined strength would announce to the community that the wedding had been performed. Then the minister said: "That is the way

187

it will be in your marriage. It will be easier if you both pull together."

Too many couples stop having fun together. But the writer of Ecclesiastes tells spouses to "have a blast in that marriage of yours—live it up!" Enjoy—don't endure your marriage—is his counseling.

You're excused from further reading to do something beautiful for the most important person in the world to you!

Help us, Lord, to keep the romance in our marriage, that love may grow and glow with the years, that indeed we will enjoy life with each other.

SEVENTY-NINE

TIME AND CHANCE

The race is not to the swift or the battle to the strong . . . but time and chance happen to them all (9:11).

It was a long awaited moment in the 1986 Olympics in Los Angeles. Premier American track star Mary Decker and Britain's speedy Zola Budd crouched, poised to spring forward from the starting line. Mary Decker had trained hard for four years for this moment. She was favored by many experts to win the gold medal in the women's mile event. Zola Budd was considered her most fierce competitor.

The gun exploded and the runners shot forward from the starting line with each establishing her early pace and strategy. But only a short distance into the race a tragic incident occurred, witnessed on TV by over 100 million people. Zola Budd cut in, Mary Decker tripped and was seen writhing in pain and agony on the sideline while another captured the gold medal. The incident unnerved Budd, who lost her stride and finished behind the medalists. A freak incident marred what was to be a great event of the Olympics. Chance turned expected gold into a gory memory. It became one of the saddest memories of international sports competition.

"Chance happens to all," writes the preacher of Ecclesiastes. An unexpected turn, an accident, an illness, or

189

one of an innumerable company of the unexpected, can turn life around in an instant. Dreams burst, hopes are dashed, plans foiled, and the gold medals of our life's quest exceed our reach forever.

"The race is not to the swift"—the swift-footed may find himself a loser. "Or the battle to the strong"—military prowess does not guarantee success in battle. "Nor does food come to the wise"—wisdom does not assure a livelihood. "Or wealth to the brilliant"—understanding does not insure prosperity. "Or favor to the learned"—skill does not ensure preference. The factors of time and chance can upset all human concepts and calculations.

Time imposes its limits upon us. We may not have enough time, or we may run out of time.

"Dost thou love life?" asked Benjamin Franklin. He answered his own question: "Then do not squander time. For that's the stuff life is made of." Time wasted is existence; used, it is life. The Roman axiom, *carpe diem,* "seize the day," is a motto for all of us to live by.

Chance, life's unexpected events, can also affect our progress and pursuits. But in life's race, God's grace enables us to go on and be winners, against even the most formidable happenings. We don't have to lie in agony on the sidelines. God has promised that "those who wait on the Lord shall renew their strength. . . . they shall run and not be weary!" (Isa. 40:31, NKJV)

We are all runners in the great marathon of life. There is a prize immeasurably greater than a gold medal. There's a victory celebration unmatched in earth's recognitions. The race is not to the swift, but it is to the saved and sanctified by the grace and Spirit of God. Wanna race?

> *Eternal God, enable us by Your Spirit to "lay aside every weight, and the sin that so easily ensnares us, and let us run with endurance the race that is set before us" (Heb. 12:1, NKJV)*

190

EIGHTY
SHARING OUR BREAD

Cast your bread upon the waters
for after many days you will find it again (11:1).

One of the memorable verses of this intriguing book speaks a timeless truth: "Cast your bread upon the waters, for after many days you will find it again."

Elijah Cadman, in the early days of The Salvation Army, had his own paraphrase of this text: "Cast your bread upon the water and it will return to you honeyed toast." What we give in life does come back to us in many rewarding ways.

Our contemporary culture is obsessed with the passion to possess. The clever G.K. Chesterton reminds his readers that there are two ways to get enough: one is to continue to accumulate more and more; the other is to desire less. Solzhenitsyn, writing from his Russian prison camp, gives his antidote for our plague of compulsive buying, urging us to "keep as few things as possible. Let memory be your travel bag." This word from the Teacher of Ecclesiastes is not a casual suggestion, but a caveat against hoarding and a mandate for unselfish giving.

This text takes on new meaning and urgency in our day. Never in history has there been such a need to share our bread. Millions across the waters are starving.

Our suffering world calls for our response of compassion and action. "The road to holiness necessarily passes through the world of action," wrote Dag Hammarskjold in his diary. We will be the poorer, for our souls will be impoverished, if we do not respond to the cries and heartaches of our world. Those who will pay the price of caring are desperately needed today.

A poet helps us express our response to Solomon's text on sharing our bread:

> The bread that bringeth strength I want to give,
> The water pure that bids the thirsty live:
> I want to help the fainting day by day;
> I'm sure I shall not pass again this way.
>
> I want to give the oil of joy for tears
> The faith to conquer crowding doubts and fears.
> Beauty for ashes may I give alway:
> I'm sure I shall not pass again this way.
>
> I want to give to others hope and faith,
> I want to do all that the Master saith;
> I want to live aright from day to day;
> I'm sure I shall not pass again this way.
>
> —Author unknown

God of love, make me an instrument of Your compassion to the hungry, the hurting, and all to whom in Your name I may give the cup of cold water or the sustaining bread.

EIGHTY-ONE
WHILE YOU ARE YOUNG

Be happy, young man, while you are young,
and let your heart give you joy
in the days of your youth (11:9).

Youth should be a time of rejoicing. That is God's plan. With this command to "be happy" the writer urges "but know that for all these things God will bring you to judgment."

Augustine perceptively expresses this same truth: "Love God, and do as you please." The Preacher of Ecclesiastes is saying, "Live life to the full." But he also reminds us that we will be accountable for what we do.

He then supplies one of the pertinent verses of the Bible for youth: "Remember your Creator in the days of your youth, before the days of trouble come and the years approach when you will say, I find no pleasure in them" (12:1).

The following prayer by J.H. Miller was published years ago in a Salvation Army youth publication. When youth today aspire to these qualities, then they will know the pleasure that comes in doing the will of God.

Lord, let my life be like a light
   That shines in every way,
To show to those sunk in sin's night
   The road to perfect day.

193

Lord, let my life be like the sea
  That comes in wave on wave,
To show Thy fullness, Lord, in me,
  Through God's great power to save.

Lord, let my life be like a book,
  Its pages all aglow.
With words of life for all who look
  And want their Lord to know.

Lord, let my life be anything,
  If it but spreads Thy fame,
Or helps a soul avoid sin's sting
  By shelt'ring 'neath Thy name.

Lord, let my life be like Thine own,
  Pure, holy, undefiled,
And never let me from Thee roam
  Or be by sin beguiled.[10]

Lord, for whom young men gave up all to follow You, bless the youth whom this moment I name before You. Help them to grow in the knowledge and love of their Lord and Savior. Kindle their imaginations with high resolve, and lead them into victorious and purposeful lives.

EIGHTY-TWO
LIFE IS FRAGILE

Remember Him before the silver cord is severed (12:6).

"Poetry begins in delight," observed Robert Frost, "and ends in wisdom." In the Teacher's masterpiece of memorable lines, two dual images depict the beauty and fragility of life.

The first dual image is that of a golden bowl suspended by a silver cord or chain. The cord becomes frayed and breaks. The golden lamp crashes in pieces on the floor. The gold and silver symbolize life's preciousness. Life is as delicately wrought as an ornamental lamp and as fragile as a piece of pottery. Death is the smashing of the bowl.

The highly figurative language continues in the second pair of images which depict a pitcher lowered into a well by a rope running round a wheel. The wheel breaks and the pitcher lies broken in the well. Death is life cut off from its source.

These images eloquently speak to us of the fragility of life. The lamp of life finally falls with a crash on the floor and its light is extinguished forever. The water pot lies broken at the source, and the water that sustains life can no longer be drawn. Life is fragile. It will someday be broken, its beauty and usefulness terminated. There will be a last step for every familiar journey, a final effort for every routine task.

The Book of Ecclesiastes is said to have the smell of the tomb about it. Yet it is not a rejection of life. Rather it affirms life, in spite of its anomalies and limitations.

"Remember Him" is the urgent plea, because life is so fragile.

> Remember Him before the silver cord is severed,
>   or the golden bowl is broken;
> before the pitcher is shattered at the spring,
>   or the wheel broken at the well (12:6).

Life is fragile. Handle with prayer.

Eternal God, help me as I pass through things temporal, not to lose that which is eternal.

EIGHTY-THREE
A REQUIEM OF MORTALITY

The dust returns to the ground where it came from, and the spirit returns to God who gave it (12:7).

This passage presents one of the Bible's most poignant descriptions of old age and death (12:2-8). Twice we are warned to remember God before time exacts its heavy toll (12:1, 6).

The "dust to dust" suggested by this text is a requiem as old as mortality, repeated in the interment of our dead. And note here the affirmation that the "spirit returns to God who gave it." Its bright ray of light penetrates the darkness of pessimism and disillusionment of these pages.

William Jennings Bryan in his lecture on "The Prince of Peace" affirmed this truth of the spirit returning to God:

If the Father designs to touch with divine power, the cold and pulseless heart of the buried acorn and make it burst forth from its prison walls, will He leave neglected in the earth the soul of a man made in the image of his Creator?

If He stoops to give to the rose bush whose withered blossoms float upon the autumn breeze the sweet assurance of another spring, will He refuse the words of hope to the sons of men when the frost of winter comes?

197

If matter, mute and inanimate, though changed by the forces of nature into a multitude of forms can never die, will the imperial spirit of man suffer annihilation when it has paid a brief visit like a royal guest to this tenement of clay?

Our bodies will, as the Teacher of Ecclesiastes states, return to dust. But gloriously true as well is his inspired insight that our spirits will return home to God. What a radiant affirmation tucked away in the pessimistic pages of this book!

Through the centuries men were puzzled, perplexed by death. It was not only a mystery but the ultimate terror. But Christ the mighty Conqueror of death changed all that. By the decisive sword thrust of His resurrection He cut the Gordian knot of death and transformed fear into faith.

Life after death is not a postscript or an appendix to the book of life. Rather it is the text, a text without end. Our earthly life merely prefaces the larger life that awaits when our spirit returns to the God who gave it.

William Barclay affirms his Christian faith for the end of life's transient journey that can well serve as an appendage to the preacher's text in Ecclesiastes: "The end of time is eternity. The end of life is God. The last step of life is the step which leads into the presence of God. What consummation!"[11]

Eternal God, when day is far spent and evening shadows fall across my path, grant a firm and courageous faith in the One who is the Resurrection and the Life and His glorious promise that I will live with Him forever.

EIGHTY-FOUR
THE RIGHT WORDS

The Teacher...
pondered and searched out and set in order many
proverbs (12:9).

An intriguing text near the close of Ecclesiastes could well make the Teacher the patron saint of writers. He writes of the partnership between thought and expression, research and teaching. He didn't just throw all these thoughts together haphazardly. He "pondered," "searched out," "set in order," and sought to find just the right words. He was careful that "what he wrote was upright and true" (12:9-10).

It is axiomatic that "hard writing makes easy reading." Because of the discipline and effort of the writer of Ecclesiastes, this book takes its place with the classic literature of the world and provides us with such picturesque paths of truths.

Christian writers summon themselves to an unremitting pursuit of excellence. Cheap literature and media constantly erode the shoreline of noble standards and holy living. God calls His writers today to be the literary salt to arrest the pollution that invades America's bookshelves and living rooms. The compelling motive for Christian excellence is in the nature of God—who He is. God Himself is perfect, supremely excellent. His marvelous creation and handiwork eloquently witness to His excellence. Thus writing becomes, as other creative expressions, an act of worship.

Philip Yancey challenges: "It's time for writers to realize that the quality of our work becomes an integral part of its message."[12] C.S. Lewis likened his role as a Christian writer to an adjective humbly striving to point to the Noun of truth. Let's improve our adjectives!

"Lines to a Writer" by Salvationist poet Catherine Baird expresses the high honor of the calling of a Christian writer:

> When strong men lie divested of their power,
>   When youth is robbed of beauty's early flower,
> When silver tones like echoes slowly die,
>   And useless riches all corroded lie—
> Thy work shall teach the beauty of His will
>   When thine own heart is cold and thy lips still;
> For unto thee, most honored among men
>   As to another one, He gave—a pen;
> His hidden secrets haloed in new Light
>   To thee He whispers, then He bids thee, "Write!"

Lord, with the psalmist I would pray, "Let the words of my mouth and the meditation of my heart be acceptable in Your sight, O Lord, my strength and my Redeemer (Ps. 19:14, NKJV).

EIGHTY-FIVE

THE FRIENDS ON OUR BOOKSHELVES

Of making many books there is no end (12:12).

"Reading maketh a full man," wrote Francis Bacon in the seventeenth century. Over two centuries later, Thoreau stated, "Many a man has dated a new era in his life from the reading of a book." John Bunyan was a pagan when he married. His wife's dowry was just two books. Bunyan read them, they changed his life, and he gave to the world his immortal *Pilgrim's Progress.* Books have had an inestimable impact upon man and history.

Through the years this truth has been attested by those who have made enduring contributions to our life and thought. When the old warrior Paul was in a damp jail cell, what was his request? He asked his friend to bring a cloak for his body and books for his mind. C.S. Lewis, who has left a peerless legacy of Christian literature, said that it was through the reading of the works of George MacDonald that he was influenced to Christ.

Richard Foster writes in *Celebration of Discipline:* "Many Christians remain in bondage to fears and anxieties simply because they do not avail themselves of the Discipline of study . . . the tenor of their lives remains unchanged. Why? Because they have never taken up one of the central ways God uses to change us: study. Jesus

201

made it unmistakably clear that it is the knowledge of the truth that will set us free."[13]

Evelyn Underhill further underscores the priority of reading: "Spiritual reading is, or at least can be, second only to prayer as a developer and support of the inner life. In it we have access to all the hoarded supernatural treasure of the race: all that it has found out about God."[14]

How bereft we would be without the friends on our bookshelves. They instruct and inspire us as they share their struggles and triumphs and encounters with God.

Today many suffer from media overload. We drown in a sea of information but starve for knowledge and truth. Allan Bloom's best-selling and seminal book, *The Closing of the American Mind,* gives a scathing indictment of our education system in which philosophical relativism and intellectual anarchy have replaced a quest for truth. "Truth is relative" and "There are no absolutes" are the moral postulates in academia. Bloom cites as a major reason for the moral and intellectual decay the fact that "students have lost the practice of and the taste for reading. . . . The notion of books as companions is foreign to them. . . . There is no printed word to which they look for counsel, inspiration or joy. . . . The failure to read good books both enfeebles the vision and strengthens our most fatal tendency—the belief that the here and now is all there is."[15] Bloom's book is as a glove thrown down at the Christian's feet. It should challenge us to action so that our children and their children will not suffer from the fallout of the system.

"A good book is the best of friends." Let us enrich our lives by a goodly company of them.

Living Word, thank You for inspiring those who have left us such a vast legacy of literature for our enrichment. Help me invest time and thought in the company of good books that I may be enriched and grow in Your knowledge and grace.

EIGHTY-SIX

VALEDICTORY

Now all has been heard;
here is the conclusion of the matter:
Fear God and keep His commandments,
for this is the whole duty of man (12:13).

Solomon comes now to the close of his memoirs and states his conclusion on life. His search for meaning in the endless halls of humanism is now over. Having been caught in the jaws of his horizontal perspective "under the sun," he gives us the clue to the mystery of life. The solution to life's riddle was reserved to the end:

For God will bring every deed into judgment,
including every hidden thing,
whether it is good or evil (12:14).

The Teacher has given us his valedictory. Its timeless message echoes across the millenniums and challenges us to live by its truth. His hard-won insight has a message for us who live "under the sun." May it lead us to the Son of God, who came to be the Light of the world and who enables us to discover life's ultimate meaning.

It is forever true that the whole duty for each of us is to revere God and keep His commandments. Trust and obedience are the keys to the meaning of life.

This timeless truth has been beautifully expressed for us in the time-honored hymn of John H. Sammis:

When we walk with the Lord
  In the light of His word,
What a glory He sheds on our way;
  While we do His good will,
  He abides with us still,
And with all who will trust and obey.

But we never can prove
  the delights of His love,
Until all on the altar we lay;
  For the favor He shows,
  And the joy He bestows,
Are for them who will trust and obey.

*Divine Shepherd, help me walk life's path in trust
and obedience to Your will.*

WORDS OF WISDOM FROM THE SONG OF SONGS

EIGHTY-SEVEN
THE INCOMPARABLE SONG

Solomon's Song of Songs (1:1).

"There is bread in these words of Solomon . . . in this book which is called 'The Song of Songs.' Let us set it before us, and break it according to our need."[1] So wrote Bernard of Clairvaux (1090–1153) in his 170,000-word introduction to his eighty-six sermons on the first two chapters of this book.

"This nuptial anthem," wrote Bernard, "is named 'Song of Songs' for its surpassing excellence." "Song of Songs" was the Hebrew way of expressing the superlative, like "Lord of lords" and kindred expressions. Of Solomon's 1,005 songs (1 Kings 4:32), this was his most eloquent. It has been called "Solomon's Incomparable Song."

Solomon is identified as the author seven times in this brief book (1:1, 5; 3:7, 9, 11; 8:11, 12).

The name of Bernard is one of the most eminent of the medieval church. We still sing his enduring hymns of devotion, "Jesus, Thou Joy of Loving Hearts," "O Sacred Head Now Wounded," "Jesus, the Very Thought of Thee," and others. Something about Solomon's Song of Songs captivated his thought and enraptured his heart. What a strange paradox that St. Bernard, a celibate monk, should leave us such a glowing discourse on the idyllic affection which he and his fellow monks had all renounced.

If such a spirit found so much in this song, then there is more than meets the eye in this book. Let us then break its bread according to our need.

Break Thou the bread of life,
Dear Lord, to me,
As Thou didst break the loaves
Beside the sea;
Beyond the sacred page
I seek Thee, Lord;
My spirit pants for Thee,
O living Word!
—Mary A. Lathbury

EIGHTY-EIGHT
A EULOGY ON LOVE

We will praise your love (1:4).

Many have found this Song of Songs difficult to understand and accept because of its erotic language and description of intimate love. But we must remember that these lines of sensuous affection come to us from an ancient oriental culture that held the relationship of lovers in highest esteem.

This book has a special message for an age that has popularized infidelity, rejected the pure instinct of love, brought marriage into disrepute, and identified lust with love.

Furthermore, biblical realism recognizes sex as intrinsically interwoven in the fabric of human nature. Sex is portrayed in the Bible as a dynamic and often dominant force in life. It is a God-given gift for the enjoyment and propagation of children.

Many avoid a study of this book due to absence of any reference to God or religious themes and the difficulty of identifying the speakers. Yet the Jews read it every year at their Passover, their most sacred feast. And devout readers of Scripture through the ages have drawn rich inspiration from its pages. Bernard of Clairvaux considered this book to "belong to the advanced and instructed soul,

which by the progress in grace . . . to be fit for the nup-
tials with its heavenly spouse."

Different schools of interpretation of the Song of Songs
boast devout and scholarly adherents. But there is an
inherent danger in an allegorical interpretation, as pointed out by Adam Clarke: "Were this mode of interpretation (the allegorical) to be applied to the Scriptures in
general, in what a state would religion soon be! Who
could see anything certain, determinate, and fixed in the
meaning of the Divine oracles, when fancy and imagination must be the standard interpreters? God has not left
His Word to man's will in this way."[2]

Clarke, of course, points out that allegory and metaphor
may be employed where clearly indicated. This writing
interprets the text as a eulogy and anthology of love lyrics;
a celebration of human love in its purity and rapture, with
spiritual application of its celebration of love.

Christianity is essentially a love affair between the believer and his Lord. With Bernard of Clairvaux, we sing:

Jesus, Thou joy of loving hearts,
Thou fount of life, Thou light of all,
From the best bliss that earth imparts,
We turn unfilled to Thee again.

Thy truth unchanged hath ever stood;
Thou savest those that on Thee call;
To them that seek Thee Thou art good,
To them that find Thee all in all.

*Jesus, tender Lover of my soul, lead me to a deeper
love and devotion, that I may love You more dearly
and follow You more nearly each passing day.*

EIGHTY-NINE
KEEPER OF THE VINEYARDS

My mother's sons were angry with me and made me the keeper of the vineyards (1:6).

The three main characters of Song of Songs are considered by most to be Solomon, the Shulamite woman—a lovely country girl—and the "daughters of Jerusalem." Modern translations helpfully identify the speakers and their sequence, making the book easier to understand. The NIV, for example, uses the titles, "Beloved," "Lover," "Friends" as captions for passages.

Beloved expresses deep longing for her lover:

Let him kiss me with the kisses of his mouth—for your love is more delightful than wine (1:2).

Wine in the Bible is often a symbol for the delights of life. She yearns for fragrances of her lover's presence and his very name makes her exude the ecstasy of love (1:3).

We now come upon a verse that should cause us to pause and ponder:

They made me the keeper of the vineyards,
But my own vineyard I have not kept (1:6, NKJV).

How often we have seen people so busy in their

church activity, doing for others, absorbed by their work, that they have neglected their own requirements of personal life and family. Sacred relationships with children or spouse have been sacrificed on the altar of activity.

Vineyards require great care, and so do our personal lives and the loved ones entrusted to us. There can either be the beauty and bounty of a harvest, or a withered vine—depending upon our priorities. This verse is a powerful preachment on "first things first."

Lord Jesus, help me live by the priorities of love and the needs of others to whom I relate.

NINETY
ROSE OF SHARON

I am a rose of Sharon,
a lily of the valleys (2:1).

This passage relates a dialogue of love in the most intimate and endearing language. The rapturous delight two
lovers find in each other is openly expressed. Lover
exclaims:

How beautiful you are, my darling!
   "Oh, how beautiful!
Your eyes are doves" (1:15).
Beloved responds:
"How handsome you are, my lover!
   Oh, how charming!
And our bed is verdant" (1:16).
Beloved describes herself:
"I am a rose of Sharon,
a lily of the valleys" (2:1).

These titles have come to be applied to our Lord in our
devotional language, singing, "He's the Lily of the Valley,"
and "Jesus, Rose of Sharon." Our Lord is as the exquisite
flower that thrives in the cool countryside or in the quiet
field. We discover His beauty when we come apart from
the hustle and bustle of life and enter into solitary and

213

sweet communion with the Lover of our souls.

In Romania there is a valley where nothing is grown but roses for the Vienna market. The perfume of the valley at the time of the rose crop is such that if you go there for even a few minutes, wherever you go the rest of the day people know you have been in the company of the roses in the valley. You carry with you its fragrance.

When we are in company with the One who is the Rose of Sharon, we will carry with us the fragrance of His presence and others will know we have been with Jesus. The fragrance of His life in ours will be passed on to others as our lives distill His beauty and winsomeness.

Let the beauty of Jesus be seen in me,
All His wonderful passion and purity.
O Thou Spirit divine, all my nature refine,
Till the beauty of Jesus be seen in me.[3]

NINETY-ONE

BANNER OF LOVE

He has taken me to the banquet hall,
and his banner over me is love (2:4).

In the distant time of our text, kings had their military banners. The banners, or ensigns of the tribes over which he ruled, flapped over Solomon's pavilion, silhouetted against the sky. Any person who lived or served under one of those banners was under the king's protection.

Beloved had a banner that meant more to her than all the king's banners. It was the banner of her lover—"his banner over me is love."

The believer in Christ also confidently exclaims, "His banner over me is love." His love protects us from sin and the onslaughts of Satan. We are under the protection of the King of Kings, the Mighty Conqueror over sin.

A story is told of a young man who was born in England, became a naturalized U.S. citizen, and went to live in Cuba for a while. When the civil war broke out in Cuba in 1867, he was arrested as a spy, taken before the Spanish military court, and ordered shot. The English and American consuls believed in his innocence and pleaded for his release, but the Spaniards haughtily disregarded their petition. He was given no time for an appeal, and as the hour of execution arrived, the condemned English-American stood at the foot of the grave dug for him, his hands tied behind him, and the black cap drawn over his head. The officer ordered his men to load, and at the word "present" they brought their rifles to their shoulders, awaiting the command to fire. Then suddenly there sprang forward from the bystanders the two consuls. One threw over the prisoner the Stars and Stripes and the other draped over him the Union Jack. The consuls stood with the prisoner, defying the Spaniards, who dared not fire on the flags of two of the mightiest nations under heaven. The man later proved his innocence and was released.

There is security for the Christian who is under the blood-stained banner of the Cross. May we know the divine communion spoken of by the inspired poet of old, "He has taken me to the banquet hall" and may we joyously witness to His sheltering care, "His banner over me is love."

Love divine, all loves excelling,
Joy of heaven, to earth come down,
Fix in us Thy humble dwelling,
All Thy faithful mercies crown.
Jesus, Thou art all compassion,
Pure, unbounded love Thou art;
Visit us with Thy salvation,
Enter every longing heart.

Finish then Thy new creation,
Pure and spotless let us be;
Let us see Thy great salvation,
Perfectly restored in Thee.
Changed from glory into glory,
Till in heaven we take our place,
Till we cast our crowns before Thee,
Lost in wonder, love and praise.
—Charles Wesley

NINETY-TWO
LOVE'S VULNERABILITY

I am lovesick (2:5, NKJV).

Suddenly a minor chord is introduced in our love song and will recurringly be heard. As is so well known, all is not smoothness and sweetness in the course of love. We hear from these pages the plaintive sigh, "I am lovesick."

There is always a counterpoint of deep pathos that vibrates to the delightful passions of love. Beloved is here expressing the pang and heartache of separation. To love is to embark on the most vulnerable experience in the world. With its ecstasies also come its deep hurts and sorrows. The greatest love ever known to man had its Calvary and cross.

No one ever said it better than C.S. Lewis: "To love at all is to be vulnerable. Love anything, and your heart will certainly be wrung and possibly be broken. If you want to make sure of keeping it intact, you must give your heart to no one, not even to an animal. Wrap it carefully round with hobbies and little luxuries; avoid all entanglements; lock it up safe in the casket or coffin of your selfishness. But in that casket — safe, dark, motionless, airless — it will change. It will not be broken; it will become unbreakable, impenetrable, irredeemable."[4]

Our love for the Lord may very well be proven by how

217

much we have sacrificed and suffered for Him. Amy Carmichael has expressed it poignantly:

> Hast thou no scar?
> No hidden scar on foot, or side, or hand?
> I hear thee sung as mighty in the land,
> I hear them hail thy bright ascendant star,
> Hast thou no scar?
>
> Hast thou no wound?
> Yet I was wounded by the archers, spent,
> Leaned Me against a tree to die; and rent
> By ravening beasts that compassed Me, I swooned:
> Hast thou no wound?
>
> No wound, no scar?
> Yet, as the Master shall the servant be,
> And, pierced are the feet that follow Me;
> But thine are whole; can he have followed far
> Who has no wound or scar?[5]

Divine Love, surpassing understanding and wounded for my transgressions, I give my dearest and my best, all that I am and hope to be, to the call of Your infinite love.

NINETY-THREE
THE GREATEST NEWS

Behold, he comes (2:8, NKJV).

The exuberance of Lover's approach is vibrantly portrayed in Beloved's ecstasy:

> The voice of my beloved!
> Behold, he comes
> Leaping upon the mountains,
> Skipping upon the hills (2:8, NKJV).

Those who interpret Song of Songs as an allegory of the
relationship of love between the Lord and the Christian
find here a foreshadowing of our Lord's return. "Behold,
He is coming!" is the promise of the last book of the Bible
(Rev. 22:7). Thus, allegorists see in this Old Testament
text the ecstasy of His coming as His beloved exclaims,
"Behold, he comes!"

When we hear the media news of our day, we say,
"The worst is yet to come." But, when we read the Bible,
we say, "The best is yet to be." No less than 318 verses in
the 216 chapters of the New Testament refer to our Lord's
second coming. One in 30 verses points forward with
eager gestures to His return. All nine new Testament authors herald His second advent.

Our creeds affirm the tumultuous truth, many echoing the Nicene creed, "He shall come again with glory." Our hymns exult in its anticipation with 5,000 of Charles Wesley's 7,000 hymns referring to the doctrine. In our day, the Gaithers have lyricized for us to sing, "The King is coming!"

The second coming of Jesus Christ will be the coronation and culmination of all history. When the believer says, "Behold, He comes!" it will be his crowning joy.

Thank You, Jesus, for Your great and glorious promise that You are coming again. Grant that by Your grace and the Holy Spirit I will be longing and living and ready for Your triumphant return.

NINETY-FOUR

A SPRINGTIME LYRIC

For lo, the winter is past (2:11, NKJV).

The coming of the *beloved* is associated with the bursting forth of springtime as described in one of the delightful stanzas of "Solomon's Incomparable Song":

> My beloved spoke, and said to me:
> "Rise up, my love, my fair one,
> And come away.
> For lo, the winter is past,
> The rain is over and gone.
> The flowers appear on the earth;
> The time of singing has come,
> And the voice of the turtledove
> Is heard in our land.
> The fig tree puts forth her green figs,
> And the vines with the tender grapes
> Give a good smell.
> Rise up, my love, my fair one
> And come away!" (2:10-13, NKJV)

H.A. Ironside, writing on this text, gives an inspiring application: "Does it not stir your soul to think that at any moment we may hear His voice saying, 'Arise, my love, and come away? . . . We shall rejoice together, when earth's long winter of sorrow and trial and perplexity is ended and the glorious spring will come with our blessed Lord's return. . . .' This is a complete love-lyric in anticipation of the bridegroom's return. How soon He may come for whose hearts yearn for Him, we do not know. We have waited for Him through the years; we have known the cold winters . . . but oh, the joy, the gladness when He comes back!"[6]

We have here an inspired lyric on the beauty of nature and, in particular, the springtime. Spring breaks forth in song with "the voice of the turtledove," a migratory bird that heralds the spring in Palestine with its appearance. Nature bursts with new life in the glory of springtime.

The fragrance and loveliness of pastoral scenes and life impregnate this song. Our senses are stimulated by clusters of henna blossoms, fir trees and cedars, the rose of Sharon and the lilies of the valley, raisin cakes and apples, myrrh and frankincense, oils and spices, pomegranates, saffron and calamus and cinnamon, nectar, flocks and vineyards, doves and little foxes, young stags and gazelles, flocks of goats and hinds of the field, the flowing streams of Lebanon.

This poem in praise of love transports us back to the clean fresh fragrance and the refreshing loveliness of the outdoors, all too often lost in our urban lifestyles. We too, upon return to the beauty and wonder of nature, may find a tryst and communion with the Lover of our soul.

Perhaps we need to hear His voice during our earthly tasks and struggles, saying, "Arise, my love, and come away."

> *Dear Savior, thank You for the springtime You have brought to my soul, for the new life and invigoration and the song You put in my heart when You came and said, "Arise, my love, and come away."*

NINETY-FIVE
THE LITTLE FOXES

Catch us the foxes,
the little foxes that spoil the vines,
for our vines have tender grapes (2:15, NKJV).

A landmark of truth meets us on our journey through this love lyric. Our relationship of love with our Lord is a tender one, requiring the utmost vigilance against those things that would hurt and destroy. There are many "little foxes" that would spoil the vine. It can happen ever so slyly, subtly, swiftly—if we are not on guard. The little foxes will come into our spiritual vineyard through carelessness or neglect.

The text warns us to beware of the "little" things. The large foxes are more easily detected and driven off. But it is the little things that often make a difference in a relationship of love. A little remembrance, or a little forgetfulness. A little word of carelessness, or a little word of tenderness. A little compromise with the world, little indulgences of the flesh, little neglects of duty—and the beauty and fruitfulness of the vine are sacrificed.

For want of a nail the shoe was lost;
For want of a shoe the horse was lost;
For want of a horse the rider was lost;
For want of a rider the battle was lost;
All for want of a little nail.[7]

It is usually not the big things of life that cause us the most trouble and defeat. They call forth our resources and the support of others and we get through them. But the small everyday encounters and tests of our faith often make the difference. The little things that make up our everyday determine our conduct and character and destiny. Let us beware of the "little foxes" that can spoil the tender vines of our lives.

God of the galaxies, I praise You because You are also the God of the infinitely small things that make up my finite life. Help me not to let the "little foxes" spoil the tender vine of my life and fruitfulness for You.

NINETY-SIX
THE BOND OF LOVE

My beloved is mine, and I am his (2:16, NKJV).

This key verse expresses the theme of Song of Songs, a beautiful expression of love which is repeated in 6:3 and 7:10. True love creates a bonding, a belonging. How reassuring to know that we belong to our Lord and He belongs to us. With songwriter Norman J. Clayton, we exult in song:

> Now I belong to Jesus,
> Jesus belongs to me,
> Not for the years of time alone,
> But for eternity.[8]

How long is this intimate relationship to last?

> Until the day breaks
> And the shadows flee (2:17).

We may spiritualize this text in applying it to that blessed new day of the Lord's coming when all earthly shadows shall forever flee, when there will be no more night or darkness, and He Himself will be our light (Rev. 21:23-25).

Once more we hear the strains of a minor chord sounding in this love lyric:

> I sought the one I love;
> I sought him, but I did not find him (Song 3:1, NKJV).

The *beloved* is separated from and longs for the *lover*. She looks diligently for him and again sighs, "I sought him, but I did not find him" (3:2).

But the king is coming in all his royal splendor and power (3:6-11). He is coming to take to himself his bride and consummate their marriage.

Lover speaks to his love in the most endearing terms, with fervent admiration for her exquisite beauty:

> Behold, you are fair, my love. . . .
> You have ravished my heart
> With one look of your eyes (4:1, 9, NKJV).

In his torrent of passion, Lover chooses the most striking beauties and precious treasures to serve as similes and metaphors of his love (4:1–5:1).

How precious and beautiful is the joy of being bonded to Christ eternally by the Cross and His infinite love.

Jesus, I love You.

NINETY-SEVEN
LOVE'S EXTRAVAGANCE

My lover is . . . outstanding among ten thousand (5:10, NKJV).

Another "dark night of the soul" intrudes upon the song (5:2-9) before the devoted ardor reasserts itself in describing the lover. Some of her poetic phrases have found their way into our hymns in association with our Lord: "Chief among ten thousand" (5:10), and "He is altogether lovely" (5:16).

The love lyric rises to a crescendo of extravagant and uninhibited reveling in physical charms (5:10–7:13). In one of the more conservative expressions, Lover responds to Beloved who to him is as:

Fair as the moon,
Clear as the sun,
Awesome as an army with banners (6:10, NKJV).

In one of our songs of devotion by Edward Joy, we sing of the Lover of our souls:

Jesus, tender Lover of my soul,
    Pardoner of my sins, and Friend indeed,
Keeper of the garden of my heart,
    Jesus, Thou art everything to me.

227

What to me are all the joys of earth?
   What to me is every sight I see,
Save the sight of Thee, O Friend of mine?
   Jesus, Thou art everything to me.[9]

One of the great needs of our Christian experience is to realize the breadth and depth of God's love for us as individuals. Bible writers proclaimed the love of God in immortal words, the most renowned being, "For God so loved the world that He gave His one and only Son, that whoever believes in Him shall not perish but have eternal life" (John 3:16). Lyricists have resonated its theme in verses that have been sung around the world, such as Charles Wesley's eloquent verse: "Love surpassing understanding, / Angels would the mystery scan, / Yet so tender that it reaches / To the lowest child of man. / Let me, Jesus, fuller know redemption's plan." All our superlatives fall prostrate before the indescribable love of God.

Divine Spendthrift on my behalf, who has created with such abandonment the marvels of the world and lavished such love upon me, keep me captive to Your extravagant love.

NINETY-EIGHT

"AS STRONG AS DEATH"

Place me like a seal over your heart,
  like a seal over your arm;
for love is as strong as death,
  its jealousy unyielding as the grave.
It burns like blazing fire,
  like a mighty flame.
Many waters cannot quench love;
  rivers cannot wash it away.
If one were to give
  all the wealth of his house for love,
  it would be utterly scorned (8:6-7).

This lovely lyric climaxes with a doxology to love, in poetry of a high order.

Beloved enters into the covenant of love with a plea for the sealing of their nuptial vows. In that day, a signet worn on the hand or arm was a memorial of love, much like a wedding ring today. We need sacred reminders of our vows, the commitment and permanence of our relationships.

If one verse were singled out as the greatest of this book, it would most likely be "love is as strong as death." Here we have the apex of the eulogy to love. Death is the great destroyer. It puts an end to all things. But our love lyric declares that "love is as strong as death." Love is invincible. It cannot be vanquished by death. It transcends all barriers, including the end of life itself.

This great truth finds an echo in the enduring sonnet of Elizabeth Barrett Browning:

> How do I love thee? Let me count the ways.
> I love thee to the depth and breadth and height
> My soul can reach . . .
> I love thee purely, as they turn from Praise.
> I love thee with the passion put to use
> In my old griefs, and with my childhood's faith.
> I love thee with a love I seemed to lose
> With my lost saints—I love thee with the breath,
> Smiles, tears, of all my life!—and, if God choose,
> I shall but love thee better after death.

However, we must carry our text beyond its time. In the light of the New Testament and the Resurrection of our Lord, we confidently declare that love is stronger than death! Christ the Mighty Conqueror defeated death. With the Apostle Paul, we can rejoice in the fact that nothing can separate us from the love of God, not even death (Rom. 8:37-39).

Sovereign Lord, I praise You for Your invincible love that has conquered death and the grave, and for Your gift of eternal life through Your redeeming work on Calvary and Your mighty Resurrection.

NINETY-NINE

LOVE'S YEARNING

Many waters cannot quench love (8:7).

Our text speaks of the "unyielding jealousy" of love. The Ten Commandments teach us that God is a jealous God. Someone has said, "Love is only genuine as long as it is jealous." Because God loves us so much He does not want to see us turning away from His love and seeking satisfaction in lesser affections which can only bring harm and death. Because love cares, it is jealous, not with a selfish, but with a holy jealousy.

"Many waters cannot quench love." Those who pass through deep waters find the love of God to be adequate to carry them through, to keep them from being overcome.

Love is priceless. It cannot be bought with any sum (8:7b). It is of surpassing value.

As we come near to the close of our study of this song, we include this perceptive and helpful summary statement from *The Wesleyan Bible Commentary:*

> Some students of Scripture have felt that it was sacrilegious to look upon a portion of Scripture as given simply to celebrate the dignity and purity of human love. Perhaps this is to underestimate the divine esti-

mate of the marriage relation . . . the high place in
the divine plan that marriage was intended to play. Is
it not appropriate that in a day when sex has become a commodity and persons have become ob-
jects, when hell has appropriated sex as if it created
it, and has demanded its price for dispensing this
gift, when sex has become such an end in itself that
perversion receives the premium, that in the Scriptures there is a picture of this crucial phase of life as
God intended it to be? Perhaps an understanding of
pure love, of this phase of God's plan for man as it
ought to be, is a means of opening us to appreciate
him who is LOVE itself.[10]

Our love song closes on an expectant note: "Come
away, my lover" (8:14).

How beautiful that this delightful love song, which
many allegorize as depicting the relation between Christ
and the Christian, ends on the same note as the last book
in the Bible, calling for a quick return of the One who is
loved supremely (Rev. 22:20).

We would pray, with another, in the same yearning of
our text, "Come in all your vigor and splendor of that
boundless life of yours. Come! Leap over all obstacles!
Let nothing ever come between us again. Even so, come
Lord Jesus."

Let us approach the end our study, as we began it, with
a quote from the great work of Bernard of Clairvaux,
"Jesus, the Very Thought of Thee":

The love of Jesus,
What it is,
None but His loved ones know!

*Thank You, God, for Your boundless love that has
redeemed me, that enfolds me daily in Your care,
and someday will receive me unto Yourself.*

ONE HUNDRED
LOVE UNQUENCHABLE

Many waters cannot quench love;
rivers cannot wash it away (8:7).

In lyricizing the superiority of love, the poet exclaims, "If one were to give all the wealth of his house for love, it would be utterly scorned" (8:7). Love is the *summum bonum*, the *ne plus ultra*, the highest good, the greatest thing in the world. No earthly possessions or gifts can compare with love.

Love enriches life beyond anything else. With Tennyson's Ulysses we all must say, "I am a part of all that I have met." Others who have loved and encouraged us have made indelible impacts upon our lives. An anonymous poet has eulogized this facet of love:

I love you,
Not only for what you are,
But for what I am
When I am with you.

I love you,
Not only for what
You have made of yourself,
But for what
You are making of me.

I love you
For the part of me
That you bring out;
I love you
For putting your hand
Into my heaped-up heart
And passing over
All the foolish, weak things
That you can't help
Dimly seeing there,
And for drawing out
Into the light
All the beautiful belongings
That no one else had looked
Quite far enough to find.

I love you because you
Are helping me to make
Of the lumber of my life
Not a tavern,
But a temple;
Out of the works
Of my every day
Not a reproach,
But a song. . . .

When we apply this beautiful truth to our relationship with Christ, it takes on transcendent meaning. We love God not only for what He is but for what we are because of His love toward us and what He is making of us.

In one of the most sublime texts of the Bible, the Apostle John declares the stupendous truth:

How great is the love the Father has lavished on us, that we should be called children of God! . . . God is love. This is how God showed his love among us: He sent His one and only Son into the world that we

234

might live through Him. This is love: not that we loved God, but that He loved us and sent His Son as an atoning sacrifice for our sins. . . . We love because He first loved us (1 John 3:1; 4:8-10, 19).

The enduring, unquenchable love of God has been eloquently penned in the lyric of F.M. Lehman:

The love of God is greater far
Than tongue or pen can ever tell;
It goes beyond the highest star,
And reaches to the lowest hell.
The guilty pair, bowed down with care,
God gave His Son to win;
His erring child He reconciled,
And pardoned from his sin.

Could we with ink the ocean fill,
And were the skies of parchment made,
Were every stalk on earth a quill,
And every man a scribe by trade,
To write the love of God above
Would drain the ocean dry.
Nor could the scroll contain the whole,
Though stretched from sky to sky.

O love of God, how rich and pure!
How measureless and strong!
It shall for evermore endure
The saints' and angels' song.[11]

Heavenly Father, thank You for loving the world with such infinite love that You gave Your Son as a sacrifice for our salvation. I praise You that Calvary included me and that You have redeemed and accepted me into the eternal family of God.

Notes

Effort has been made to discover sources and obtain permission where necessary for quotations used in this book. In the event of any unintentional omission, or inability to trace sources, upon these being pointed out, due acknowledgments will be gladly incorporated in any future editions.

Proverbs

1. "Preface," *Living Psalms and Proverbs* (Wheaton, Ill.: Tyndale, 1967). (Taylor and Graham quotes.)

2. Charles R. Swindoll, *Proverbs Bible Guide* (Waco, Texas: Word, 1980), p.1.

3. John Keats, *Letter to George and Georgiana Keats.* 14 February 1819.

4. Charles Fritsch, *The Interpreter's Bible*, ed. George Buttrick et al. (Nashville: Abingdon, 1955), vol. 4, p. 781.

5. Marlene Chase, "The Single Eye," *The War Cry*, 13 October 1990, p. 8

6. Richard J. Foster, *Money, Sex & Power* (San Francisco: Harper & Row, 1985), p. 60.

7. Arthur Arnott, "Home Is Home, However Lowly," stanza 1, by permission of The Salvation Army.

8. Samuel Logan Brengle, *Helps to Holiness* (New York: Salvationist, 1896), p. 74.

9. Foster, *Money, Sex & Power*, p. 5.

10. Leslie Taylor Hunt, "All My Best Works Are Naught," stanza 3, by permission of The Salvation Army.

11. Charles T. Fritsch, "The Gospel in the Book of Proverbs," ed. John A. Mackay, *Theology Today*, vol. 7, p. 181.

12. Henry Gariepy, *100 Portraits of Christ* (Wheaton, Ill.: Victor, 1987), p. 22.

13. Robert Browning, "The Ring and the Book," line 1236.

14. James Russell Lowell, "The Present Crisis," 1844.

15. R. Laird Harris, "Proverbs," *The Wycliffe Bible Commentary* (Chicago: Moody, 1962), p. 566.

16. C.S. Lewis, *The Four Loves* (New York: Harcourt Brace Jovanovich, 1960), p. 169.

17. William Shirer, *Pastor Neimoller* (New York: Doubleday, 1959).

18. Richard J. Foster, *Celebration of Discipline* (San Francisco: Harper & Row, 1978), pp. 1, 3.

19. Ibid, p. 9.

20. National Highway Traffic Safety Admin., "National Safety Council and F.B.I. Uniform Crime Reports," 1988.

21. Dag Hammarskjold, *Markings* (New York: Alfred A. Knopf, 1964), p. 122.

22. Richard Slater, "I Have Not Much to Give Thee, Lord," by permission of The Salvation Army.

23. E. Stanley Jones, *The Divine Yes* (Nashville: Abingdon, 1975), p. 148.

24. Henry Gariepy, *Portraits of Perseverance* (Wheaton, Ill.: Victor, 1989), pp. 81–82.

25. Annie Dillard, *Pilgrim at Tinker Creek* (New York: Harper & Row, 1974), pp. 9, 135, 137.

26. Ralph Waldo Emerson, *Letters and Social Aims* (n.p., 1875).

27. *The Prayers of Peter Marshall,* ed. Catherine Marshall, (New York: McGraw-Hill, 1949), p. 170.

28. Agnes Heathcote, "Jesus Came with Peace to Me," refrain, by permission of The Salvation Army.

29. Alexander Pope, *An Essay on Man, Epistle 1*, line 1.

30. R.H. McDaniel, "Since Jesus Came into My Heart."

31. Charles W. Colson, *Born Again* (Old Tappan, N.J.: Chosen, 1976), pp. 112–13.

32. Robert Browning, *Bishop Blougram's Apology* (1855).

33. Page Smith, as quoted in *Reflections for Women Alone* by Carole Streeter (Wheaton, Ill.: Victor, 1987), pp. 48–49.

34. Mary J. Miller, "Grandmothers," *The War Cry*, 8 May 1982, used with permission.

35. Norman Cousins, *Anatomy of an Illness* (New York: A.W. Norton, 1979).

36. Pindar (c. 518–438 B.C.), *Nemean Odes, IV*, line 1.

37. E. Stanley Jones, *Christian Maturity* (Nashville: Abingdon, 1957), p. xii.

38. Robert Browning, *Rabbi Ben Ezra*, stanza 1, (1864).

39. M. Scott Peck, *The Road Less Traveled* (New York: Simon & Schuster, 1978), p. 21.

40. Dorothy Nolte, as quoted in *Children Are Wet Cement* by Anne Ortlund (Old Tappan, N.J.: Revell, 1981), p. 58, reprinted with permission.

41. Alvin Toffler, *Future Shock* (New York: Random House, 1970), p. 43.

42. Henry Wadsworth Longfellow, *A Psalm of Life*.

43. Harry David, "All My Heart I Give Thee," refrain, by permission of The Salvation Army.

44. Fulton Sheen, *Treasure in Clay* (New York: Doubleday, 1980), p. 300.

45. Albert Orsborn, "In the Secret of Thy Presence," stanza 1, by permission of The Salvation Army.

46. H.A. Ironside, *Proverbs* (Neptune, N.J.: Loizeaux, 1908), pp. 378–80.

47. *Collected Verse of Edgar A. Guest* (Chicago: Contemporary Books, 1934), p. 72.

48. Crawford H. Toy, *Proverbs – International Critical Commentary* (Edinburgh, 1899), p. 542.

Ecclesiastes

1. Derek Kidner, *A Time to Mourn & A Time to Dance* (Downers Grove, Ill.: InterVarsity, 1976), p. 13.
2. Gaius Glenn Atkins, *Interpreter's Bible,* vol. 5, ed. George Buttrick et al. (Nashville: Abingdon, 1956), p. 21.
3. Alexander Pope, *An Essay on Man, Epistle II.*
4. Albert Orsborn, "Fellowship with Thee," stanza 1, by permission of The Salvation Army.
5. *Mister Jones, Meet the Master: Sermons and Prayers of Peter Marshall,* ed. Catherine Marshall. Copyright 1949, 1950 by Fleming H. Revell Company. Renewed 1976, 1977 by Catherine Marshall LeSourd. Used by permission of Chosen Books/Fleming H. Revell Company, pp. 147–48.
6. Mary S. Edgar, "God Who Touchest Earth with Beauty," *The Hymn Book of the Anglican Church of Canada and the United Church of Canada,* (n.p., 1971), stanza 1, by permission of Peter David, Ltd.
7. Thomas R. Kelly, *A Testament of Devotion* (New York: Harper & Row, 1941), p. 29.
8. Bramwell Coles, "Here at the Cross," stanzas 2–3, by permission of The Salvation Army.
9. Alfred Lord Tennyson, *The Higher Pantheism,* (1869).
10. J.H. Miller, "A Corps Cadet's Prayer," *The Young Soldier,* 1948, by permission of The Salvation Army.
11. William Barclay, *Daily Celebration* (Waco, Texas: Word, 1971), p. 216.
12. Philip Yancey, *Open Windows* (Nashville: Thomas Nelson, 1985), p. 90.
13. Richard Foster, *Celebration of Discipline* (San Francisco: Harper & Row, 1978), pp. 54–55.
14. Evelyn Underhill, *The House of the Soul and Concerning the Inner Life* (Winston/Seabury Press, 1926).

15. Allan Bloom, *The Closing of the American Mind* (New York: Simon and Schuster, 1987), pp. 62–64.

Song of Songs

1. Bernard of Clairvaux, *Song of Solomon* (Klock & Klock Publishers, 1895), p. 7.
2. Adam Clarke, *The Holy Bible with a Commentary and Critical Notes* (New York: Abingdon-Cokesbury, n.d.), vol. 3, p. 845.
3. Albert Orsborn, "Let the Beauty of Jesus Be Seen in Me," by permission of The Salvation Army.
4. C.S. Lewis, *The Four Loves* (New York: Harcourt Brace Jovanovich, 1960), p. 169.
5. Amy Carmichael, "Toward Jerusalem," by permission of Christian Literature Crusade.
6. H.A. Ironside, *Song of Solomon* (Neptune, N.J.: Loizeaux, 1933), p. 40.
7. George Herbert, *Jacula Prudentum* (1651).
8. Norman J. Clayton, "Now I Belong To Jesus," refrain, used with permission from *Word of Life Melodies, No. 1.*
9. Edward Joy, "Jesus, Thou Art Everything to Me," stanzas 1–2, by permission of The Salvation Army.
10. Dennis Kinlaw, *The Wesleyan Bible Commentary*, vol. 2, ed. Charles W. Carter (Grand Rapids: Eerdmans, 1968), p. 657.
11. F.M. Lehman, "The Love of God," by permission of Nazarene Publishing House.